The Stones

A History in Cartoons

For Brian, Charlie, Keith,
Mick, Mick T., Stu and Woody
– we all liked a good laugh!

The Stones

A History in Cartoons

Bill Wyman
and Richard Havers

SUTTON PUBLISHING

Sutton Publishing Limited
Phoenix Mill · Thrupp · Stroud
Gloucestershire · GL5 2BU

First published 2006
Reprinted 2006

British Library Cataloguing in Publication Data
A catalogue record for this book is available from the British Library.

Every effort has been made to trace copyright holders.
Sutton Publishing apologises for any unintentional omissions and would
be pleased, if any such case should arise, to add an appropriate
acknowledgement in future editions.

ISBN 0-7509-4248-7

Page design by Glad Stockdale.

Typeset in 11/18pt Eurostile Condensed
Typesetting and origination by
Sutton Publishing Limited.
Printed and bound in England by
J.H. Haynes & Co. Ltd, Sparkford.

Contents

Introduction

Has there ever been a band that has supplied cartoonists and caricaturists with more inspiration than the Stones? Of course there have been countless performers that have had their moment under the artist's pen or brush, but no one has come in for so much ink as we have! It's not just a matter of longevity either. Cartoonists were attracted to us when we first appeared on the scene because we were different from other bands – we were five very identifiable characters. There was also the fact that our hair was longer, our clothes didn't match the stereotype 'group uniform' and in Mick we had such a recognisable front man.

Looking back through the decades of cartoons that I have collected from all over the world it is fantastic to see the many different ways in which people drew and lampooned us. Sometimes it was the things we did that got their attention, other times things we said – but as often as not it was just because we were different.

This selection of cartoons is not supposed to be definitive, nor does it set out to tell the whole story of the band. What it will do is to give people an insight into some of the funnier moments in the band's story, and simultaneously it will honour some of the world's best and most talented artists. As far as I know no other band has ever had anything like this produced about them, and I doubt that they ever will again!

I hope you enjoy this book as much as I have done in putting it together. For me to look back over five decades of events, incidents and stories that inspired some of these cartoons has reminded me of great days and wonderful times.

Bill Wyman
Suffolk, January 2006

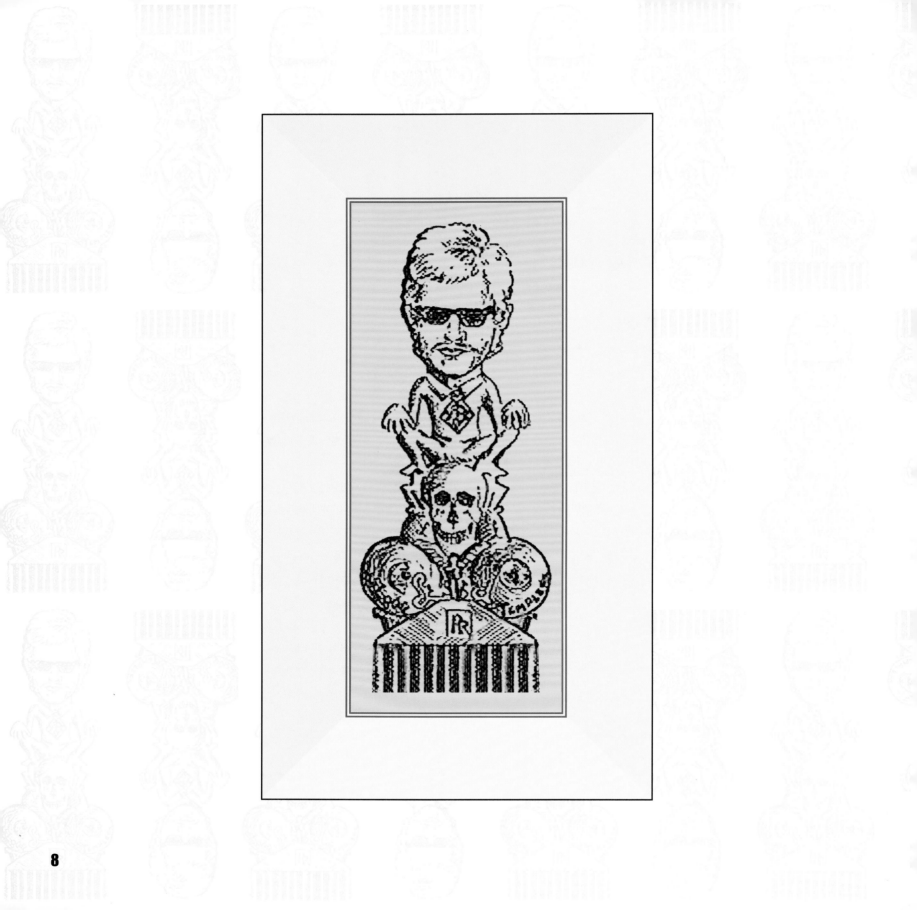

Foreword

by andrew oldham

the rolling stones are a joke . . . BUT, they also remain a way of life. bill wyman has assembled within these pages more than forty years of cartoons, 'THE STONES – a history in cartoons', the big joke being the collection, while the group is only a few years short of being fifty years old. this is not bad for a group of people who doled and dolled up the music business as a way of not having to get a regular job, getting laid regularly and seeing the world as it existed then.

the UK at the beginning of the '60s acquired two things that changed its future – the birth control pill and american music. we had something we could fantasise to, something to dance to without the inconvenience of having to settle down once we'd got what we were dancing for. american music was the compensation we war babes got for our parents and those damn yankees winning the war. for me and the likes of john lennon it was johnny ray, elvis, eddie cochran and gene vincent – for brian jones and for the other early stones it was chuck berry, muddy waters and bo diddley. for all of us it was little richard, the everly brothers and buddy holly.

england was strange and america was lucky. It seemed brits were not allowed to while americans were well endowed to. jack good introduced sex and rock 'n' roll onto our BBC screens and into our hearts. drugs were a slowtrain comin', a long way zoloft. cliff richard and billy fury were the bette davis and olivia de havilland way before whatever happened, baby, to or lady jane. they introduced songs on jack good's TV shows, 'oh, boy!' and 'boy meets girl' that the BBC would not allow us to hear. they sang those american lyrics about boy meets girl, boy can afford car to get girl and helped us nourish our dreams and escape from hell. the young ones were not allowed to see elvis from the waist up or down but when cliff sang 'one night' and billy fury suggested anything on live TV there was really no reason for elvis to leave home.

in the end the BBC could not contain us and the beatles escaped to hamburg; the stones found each other closer to home. in soho, eel pie island and richmond. long john baldry and alexis korner were the ramblin', gamblin' aunt and uncle that bet their life on the blues. georgio gomelsky was the barnum and bailey who shouted up and housed the birth of these british blues in a series of clubs behind pubs that would in short and tall order separate the toys from the girls.

cartoons about pre-'63 rock 'n' roll were few and far between. just the odd cartoon about a rock 'n' roll star getting dragged into the army, having a nervous breakdown, and that sort of thing. anyway how could you cartoon something that for the most part was a joke already. only cliff & the shadows stood strong and set the electric example of what rock would become.

then our world started combing its hair forward and writing its own songs, a sorta pre mel brooks 'producers' springtime, but brit-bred rock 'n' roll actually became an attitude; a threat to another way of life. the BBC was still a bunch of gay, as in happy, ex-RAF wankers, alleged and without prejudice of course, and they refused to play the very first stones 45 rpm. but soon we were all on the charts, it was almost walt disney on LSD. you did not know anyone who was not in the top 50, or who had a friend who managed someone who was in the top 10. that was the swinging '60s, dear friends, and that's when the cartoons started swinging as well.

the beatles were kinda off-limits, there were cartoons set around them, but not that many about them. they were the dog the master had let in the house. i mean how could you joke about, or even quote john lennon saying to the daily express's judith simons, 'if you ask me one more stupid question, judith, i'll kick you in the c***.' no, there was to be no shaking of the foundation or rattling of the jewellery. and that's the way God and PR planned it. the beatles were divined and the stones became your best hope from hell. your parent's nightmare and your cartoonist's next round down at the pub. so while this charming edition of the '60s drew to an 'archers'-like close the beatles allegedly smoked pot in the palace and got honoured, alas not blackman, while the rolling stones were roaming the yard, pissing in the moat that they would soon own.

the second half and end of the '60s was a different story. a feeding frenzy that left no stone unturned. i had by now left that circus. poland had been taken by the workers and over a couple of borders, joan of arc, also known as brian jones, had died. as had the '60s. john peel introduced real music, notchur rock 'n' roll showbiz gits, to the workers and the loser was hope and imagination, the winners football, brown ale and the smiths next door, and thus begun the great brit-slide. the stones, as their good fortune would have it, didn't have one. their money had stayed in america, some would say with americans. in any event, like all sensible paupers they headed for the south of france where they began their second golden run, this time striking the vein of more than spanish tony, or french fries at the smack cafe in marseilles, this time, they struck platinum and became the greatest rock 'n' roll band in the world. some would say that was easy given that the first had stopped touring after a nip, tuck and yank.

the cartoonists had a field day on the life and times, and perceived wealth of the stones. the stones had a field day playing the fields of altamont and giving the '60s their final death knell before joining led zep in opening up the stadiums to the future of rock 'n' roll. mick taylor played with keith like byron cooked for shelley. they captured the innocence, the skill and imagination of the early brian jones fused rolling stones. led zeppelin may have played 'stairway to heaven' but it was the stones who climbed it. it must have been frighteningly awesome, playing like the gods while still on earth, almost too heady for what was, after all, only room-serviced mortals, so mick taylor looked to the future which decided he had to go. the rolling stones came down to earth with what would become a bigger bang – ronnie wood and the yard got wider as the stones, ironically, took on a cartoon look in the '80s that had seemed so cruelly drawn in their young '60s. they became the joke they had rebelled against in their growing years; the panto and summer season that never ends – that feeling of being real and ridiculous except when you have the world in your hand – on stage or when somebody, the camera or the crowd, loves you. but that is for them to know and you to forget, for you pays yer money and you gets your pleasure. you get to go home while the real workers, those little '60s rock 'n' roll devils who thought they'd managed to avoid a regular job, have the tent packed up and moved to the next town without even pressing the elevator button or hearing the latest iraq body count.

there is hope on the cartoon front while bono tours and at least manages to get out without ed bradley from '60 minutes'. otherwise it's live at the senate for what's left of rock at the top. revisionism, halos and henna when it used to be red's song, 'cigareets, whisky and wild, wild women'. bono got to break bread with the late johnny cash, i read, and john, as he's known, asked everyone to sit still for prayers. hands held, prayers said john looked up and said to bono, 'but i sure do miss the drugs'. because he surely knew what bono didn't.

while being funny and/or cruel the cartoon has always served a social purpose, even if it's callous, witty and/or demeaning. first of all, in varying degrees, it gives us hope, release, a chuckle or a big side-splitting laugh. it's a way of getting away from envy, and our own unsettled lot, and having a damn good laugh at the expense of what we are not. it also allows us to look back not so much on the brunt of the joke – in this case the rolling stones, and have not only a hopefully full length chuckle, but via your guide throughout the years, the rockin' shakespeare (our pal, friends with gwyneth and kenneth, and also named bill), a look at what life was really about at the time. the rolling stones have become all our heroes, first masters of the world and then masters of their own world. we have partaken of their moments of triumph and those of doubt. even as the tabloid and public execution of the group began at the end of my run in 1967, as the stones refused to comply with the accepted image of how local heroes and winners should be, they rejected the role written for them, retreated and emerged as the living non-wavering meaning of life and music, albeit in the mortgaged oh so insured corporate in need of a 45 rpm world of today, but nonetheless a way of life that protects and nourishes them to this day. i'm sure that elevator buttons pressed for detail would inform that they get the joke. . . .

i never thought i'd be quoting the brothers gibb but i'm very pleased to be one who can truly say,

'i started a joke. . . .'

andrew loog oldham, january, MM6

dedicating this essay to tony meehan, the original drummer with cliff richard & the shadows, who provided the model upon which groups are still modelled. tony meehan, just like charlie with the stones, was the engine to that car. and what sets these cars apart is when the engine is so stylish, talented and finely tuned as was tony meehan.

andrew loog oldham met bill wyman on 28th april, 1963, had dinner with him for the first time 40 years later, co-managed and produced the rolling stones between 1963 and 1967, has written two volumes of autobiography, stoned and 2stoned and lives in bogota, colombia.

THE **Sixties**

I joined the Rolling Stones in December 1962. It was two months after The Beatles' first record had just managed to sneak into the British singles chart and I played my first gig with the blues band that Brian Jones had put together at the Star and Garter Hotel in Windsor. Unlike the rest of the Stones, but like just about every other band in Britain, I sported slicked-back hair with a quiff. In the week of my first gig with the band the 'group scene' had not yet begun to have an impact on the charts. The top five spots on the *New Musical Express*'s singles chart were occupied by Elvis at No. 1 with 'Return To Sender', Frank Ifield's 'Lovesick Blues', Rolf Harris's 'Sun Arise', Cliff Richard's 'The Next Time', and Susan Maughan's 'Bobby's Girl' was at No. 5 – back then every other pop star seemed to be called Bobby! Almost all performers on the charts were solo singers, with just The Tornados, The Shadows, The Four Seasons and The Everly Brothers being any different.

The Beatles were not the overnight sensation that some have since claimed; even their second single, 'Please Please Me', didn't make No. 1 in all the charts. It entered the UK Top 50 in the middle of January 1963, a week after Charlie Watts joined the Stones, and a couple of weeks after I got rid of my quiff and began to comb my hair forwards. Initially we played the clubs in and around London, with occasional forays into the Home Counties. It wasn't until 13th July 1963 that we played our first show away from our local area at the Alcove Club in Middlesbrough, and even then we were the support band for The Hollies. We had performed 'Come On', our first single, on ITV's *Thank Your Lucky Stars* on 7th July and three weeks later it made the charts – although it only got as high as No. 21. The week before we appeared on TV our manager, Andrew Oldham, had taken us to Carnaby Street, where we got black trousers and black and white dogtooth jackets, with black velvet collars. We also bought blue shirts, black knit ties, and blue leather waistcoats. We then went to Annello and Davide and bought black Spanish boots with Cuban heels (later called 'Beatle' boots). We wore the dogtooth jackets on *Thank Your Lucky Stars* and so the unsuspecting British public thought we were much like every other band dressed smartly in our uniforms. Gerry and the Pacemakers, Freddie and the Dreamers, Billy J. Kramer and the Dakotas, and The Swinging Blue Jeans had all beaten us to the charts. All these bands, along with The Beatles in their Dior suits, dressed identically and usually wore ties — the very model of respectability. The only thing that drew any comment after our TV appearance was the length of our hair. It was the start of an obsession on the part of the press and (older) public that was perfect fodder for cartoonists and newspaper reporters up and down the country. As one letter-writer to a music paper stated, 'It is disgraceful that long-haired louts such as these should be allowed to appear on TV. Their appearance was absolutely disgusting.'

By October we were added to the bill of a package tour starring The Everly Brothers, Bo Diddley and Little Richard. To begin with we were wearing our uniforms, although on certain gigs some of us wore the dogtooth jackets and others the waistcoats so even then we were on our way to becoming fashion anarchists. Our second single, a cover of Lennon and McCartney's 'I Wanna Be Your Man', made No. 12 at Christmas 1963, and the follow-up, 'Not Fade Away', entered the charts on 29th February 1964. A few weeks later it made No. 3 — we had arrived and things would never ever be the same again! America got its first real taste of the band in June 1964 when we did a short tour. After The Beatles and the others had established the bridgehead of the British invasion, we shocked an even more conservative America with not just our music but also our appearance.

3rd March 1964

This *Daily Mirror* cartoon drawn by Franklin relates to the annual Horse of the Year Show and was the first example of the media's obsession with the length of our hair.

"On Monday March 2nd we played the Albert Hall Theatre, Nottingham, on the John Leyton Package Tour, which also featured The Paramounts and Eden Kane. The next day we drove to Blackpool where we played two shows at Opera House. The Daily Mirror featured this cartoon that linked us to the Horse of the Year Show that was taking place in London that week."

RUMOUR THAT THE ROLLING STONES POP GROUP ARE ENTERING A SHETLAND PONY

FRANKLIN

21st March 1964

These five caricatures by Jimmy Thompson – the first ever to be drawn of us – appeared in the *Melody Maker*. In the same issue Mrs A. Watts from Redcar wrote a letter saying, 'I don't understand why, because a group of boys go on stage dressed individually, they should be labelled as scruffy. I sincerely hope the Stones go from strength to strength, and enjoy as much success as the Beatles.'

COOKE'S COMMENTARY

"... I've got a bit of a sore throat ... I'll have to mime my screams ..."

We went by van to the Leas Cliff Hall, in Folkestone, Kent. When we arrived, we heard that Mick (who was driving himself) had broken down. He finally made it in time. Our PA system also broke down early into the show. Mick tried to get the crowd going by shouting 'Are you all here?' and asking them to wave during 'Bye Bye Johnny', with very little response. The audience were terrible and fought a lot among themselves. We were happy when it was all over and we returned home. We got £250 for the show.

'Late morning two guys from *Western Scene* visited Mick's room, where they did an interview and photo session. We then met in the hotel's cocktail bar. Keith was wearing a sweater, Mick a striped sweatshirt and corduroy trousers, Stu a blue pullover, and Charlie and I were wearing coloured sweaters. We then went with Stu and the *Western Scene* guys for lunch in the Bristol's Grand Hotel restaurant – the Bordeaux Room. Head waiter Dick Court refused to let us eat there, as we had no ties and Mick didn't have a jacket. They offered us lightweight fawn jackets and maroon ties, but we walked out. We checked out and drove to the Bali Restaurant, in Park Street, and had a nice lunch of curried prawns and Cokes there. It was the first real meal we'd had for 24 hours.'

Back in 1964 it was considered absolutely necessary to wear a jacket and tie in almost any smart hotel dining-room – even in provincial towns, in fact even more so! It was not just cartoonists who became obsessed with our clothes and the length of our hair but just about everyone in Britain. The Beatles were considered 'well turned out', while we were called scruffy because we didn't conform to most people's idea of how a group should look. They wanted us to wear matching suits and ties. Even Andrew Oldham, our manager, thought it was a good idea at first, but we soon cured him of his thoughts! We were just following musical tradition, expressing new ideas to shock the older generation. Back in the fifties even Bill Haley was considered subversive by some.

Emmwood

"I THOUGHT ROLLING STONES GATHERED NO MOSS"

July 1964

After the Horse of the Year Show the next opportunity to link us with the animal kingdom came at the Smithfield Show. I'm not sure if they were likening Mick to a Highland bull for his long hair or for some other reason!

13th August 1964

This was the set of caricatures used to promote a show at the Palace Ballroom, Douglas, Isle of Man.

'Seventy girls fainted as the crowd hurled itself against a specially built timber and wire netting barrier. Soon it cracked under the strain. A double line of 24 policemen and attendants formed up to reinforce the barrier and fend off wave after wave of frantic fans. Fifty policemen had been called in from all over the island, and together with 40 attendants, they formed one of the biggest forces ever mustered there. Ambulance men worked full out, treating a stream of girls and one man for fainting, hysteria, cuts and scratches. The girls were laid out in blankets in the foyer. The first rush of teenagers began, as the Stones appeared on-stage. Young girls were crushed against the barrier and within minutes the police were hauling them out of the crush, onto the stage, and out to the first aid room. Policemen lost their helmets as they strained to prevent the barrier giving way completely.'

Daily Mail

'We played a 50-minute spot to an audience of 7,000. They had a police dog on stage to guard us, but it freaked out and had to be taken away.'

As this cartoon from *Rave* magazine shows, our hair continued to fascinate the media, especially when the Hong Kong authorities announced they were going to cut the hair of anyone who arrived with hair that was too long.

ABLE SEAMAN JAGGER with Naval hair do

New Chinese STONES fan

© RAVE MAGAZINE

We don't wanna go to Hong Kong We wanna keep our haircuts long

Closer to home, on 10th September the *Northern Daily Mail* reported that 'Eighteen-year-old Robert Rowell, an apprentice fitter, of Low Fell, Gateshead-on-Tyne, was not allowed to clock in at the Dunston-on-Tyne engineering works of Taylor Pallister and Co., because he had not obeyed an instruction to cut his Stones haircut; 30 apprentices walked out in sympathy. According to Robert Rowell, "I take pride in my hairstyle. I am a fan of the Stones. When I was told about it, I started wearing a cap, but then they seemed to pick on me. I will not get it cut on any account. I am willing to work with a hat on."'

26th September 1964

Signs of our growing popularity were everywhere. On 19th September *Jackie* magazine began running this cartoon strip, which purported to be 'our story' – but as you can imagine it featured a great deal of artistic licence. This was the second issue.

At about the same time, when *Fabulous* magazine asked me, 'Which incident would you pick from your lives as being the most memorable?' I replied, 'Being called Mademoiselle five times in one day while over in Switzerland.'

November 1964

'The Stones leer rather than smile. They don't wear natty clothes. They glower. Nobody would accuse them of radiating charm. The extraordinary thing is that more and more youngsters are turning towards them. How true is this carefully nourished picture of 5 indolent morons? They give the feeling that they really enjoy wallowing in a swill-tub of their own repulsiveness. They flick ash everywhere. Charlie, the zombie-eyed drummer has a habit of dropping cigarette ends in other people's coffee cups, before they've finished drinking. Keith is the one with the Oliver Twist face, and looks like a late straggler from the Russian front or a porter on a Siberian branch line.'

Alan Whittaker
News Of The World

This set of caricatures appeared in the *New Musical Express* on 6th November 1964 while we were in the middle of our second US tour. These 12 dates were much more successful than our first trip across the Atlantic. According to Ralph S. Locher (Mayor of Cleveland), 'Such groups do not add to the community's culture or entertainment. These groups still will be able to appear here at private halls but we do not feel we should invite this problem by making public facilities available.'

27th November 1964

Marilyn, another girls' magazine, began a story on us in October 1964; this is from the sixth issue.

In the early afternoon I went uptown and met with Mickie Most. I played him 'Goodbye Girl' as a possible song for The Nashville Teens, and he seemed to like it. Then I went to the rehearsal of a new group called The Cheynes, who Glyn Johns and I were going to produce the following week. In the evening I went to watch the recording of Radio Luxembourg's *Ready, Steady, Go!* radio show at the Marquee Jazz Club. The bill included Millie, The Honeycombs, The Shouts and Danny Williams.

The drummer with The Cheynes was Mick Fleetwood, who went on to be a founder member of Fleetwood Mac.

A week after our new single 'Little Red Rooster' had entered the UK singles chart, the *New Musical Express* ran this caricature of us. A week later the single made No. 1 and became one of the only Blues singles ever to top the charts. London Records, our US label, decided not to release it as a single in America. They thought, probably rightly, that, with its blatant sexual undertones, it would have been banned by most US radio stations. Brian's playing of the slide guitar harks back to the day Mick and Keith first heard him playing Elmore James-style slide at the Ealing Jazz Club in 1962.

December 1964

This Christmas cartoon was featured in *Rolling Stones Monthly* No. 7 and came at the end of what was an incredible year for us. We had two UK No. 1 singles and our first top ten in the UK had been 'Not Fade Away'. Having toured America twice we had made the Hot 100 four times, finally making it into the top ten with 'Time Is On My Side' in November. Add to that, package tours with The Ronettes, John Leyton, and Inez and Charlie Foxx as well as countless one-nighters up and down the country and you had a very busy life. In all we played 206 different gigs, many of which were two shows a night. On top of that there were numerous TV appearances, radio shows and recording sessions. We also had a No. 1 British album and an album that got to No. 11 in the USA.

‘ During the day we were visited by family and friends. We eventually got to bed at 4 a.m. Mick's brother Chris bought him a Gauguin reproduction, which was framed and hung in Mick and Keith's flat. Brian received a model train for Christmas. ’

1965

"Sorry, Kay K., but I don't think the Rolling Stones have a thing to worry about."

29

22nd January 1965

On 21st January 1965 we arrived at Kingsford Smith Airport, Sydney, on our first trip to Australia. The weather was overcast and the temperature was 65°F. A crowd of about 3,000 fans greeted us.

'One big policeman reflected "You know, 10 or 15 years ago we'd have lumbered those blokes on a vagrancy charge, for impersonating females.". . . Twenty police shoved and pushed. Fans were on the ground being trampled. Others piled on top of them, 5 deep. Baggage wagons and tow-trucks were hurriedly brought up to fill the breach. It was all over too soon. The fans streamed and screamed from the observation areas, to converge outside the customs exit doors. Among the spectators I found Mr. Digger Revell, the popular singer. "I am unable to believe that 5 young men would make themselves look this way for real. It is all, I believe, a gigantic hoax on us, their elders."'

TV Times Magazine, *Australia*

February 1965

Back from Australia we found that attention had switched from the length of our hair to Mick's lips, with this bizarre spoof ad that appeared in a music magazine. The caricature below, which appeared in the *Melody Maker* on 26th February, scored on both counts. It appeared on the day our new single, 'The Last Time', was released in the UK.

MICK JAGGER LIPS Order now !

Be in with the in-crowd, order now, new self adhesive, easy stick-on Mick Jagger lips, fab gear. Showbiz, yeh, yeh, rave of the week. Medium, large, small available.

Full details from your local lip dealer!

P.S.—Group singers! These lips help you get that true R. & B. feel.

24th March 1965

The 'Nigger Minstrel' tradition had begun in London's music halls in the nineteenth century and was revived by BBC TV as *The Black & White Minstrel Show* in June 1958. Given our love of the Blues and Black R&B it was especially insulting to be linked with what was already becoming an anachronism on the television. In 1967 the Campaign Against Racial Discrimination petitioned the BBC to take the programme off the air – but to no avail. It ran until July 1978. The most interesting feature of the cartoon is that they left out Keith for some reason. This cartoon appeared in *Pop Shop* on the day that Keith appeared at Bow Street Magistrate Court for three driving offences. Keith pleaded guilty to three motoring summonses: failing to produce his driving licence and insurance documents at a police station, and driving without L-plates.

This caricature came from the *Radio Luxembourg Annual* for 1966, published in time for Christmas 1965.

" **W**e left Gleneagles at 4 p.m. and were driven to Aberdeen. On the way we stopped off at a hotel in Laurencekirk, and had a great meal of sausages, eggs, bacon and chips. A 75-year-old character, Tom Carney, sang old Scots folk songs to us, while waiting for a meal to be cooked. In a broad accent he told us, 'You look awfly like lassies, but I like ye!' "

2nd July 1965

This cartoon followed a piece in a newspaper a few days earlier after Mr James Langmuir, Stipendiary Magistrate at Glasgow Central Juvenile Court, dealt with a boy who admitted breaking a shop window, near the Odeon Cinema. He said: 'I am surprised you go along and mix with the long-haired gentlemen called the Rolling Stones. What is the attraction for you? Complete morons like that. They wear their hair down to their shoulders, wear filthy clothes, and act like clowns. You buy a ticket to see animals like that? You think if people come here with their banjos and hair down to their waist, you can smash windows?'

Mr Tom Driberg, Labour MP for Barking, tabled a motion in the Commons which said: 'This house deplores the action of a Glasgow magistrate, James Landmuir, in using his privileged position to make irrelevant, snobbish, & insulting personal comment on the appearance & performance of the Stones, who are making a substantial contribution to public entertainment & the export drive.'

The Guardian

© EXPRESS NEWSPAPERS

'I don't know what it means, but it's not a bad name for a new group.'

On the 13th we played in Hamburg and on the 15th, Berlin. This is what the *Los Angeles Times* had to say: 'West Berlin licked its wounds after the Stones passed through. They left behind them property damage of at least $100,000, 85 arrested, and 73 injured, including 12 policemen. A police horse also was injured. Boys and girls set fires, disrobed and fought police inside and outside the stadium. Outside, teenagers damaged automobiles, harassed passers-by and damaged at least 17 cars of the Communist-run elevated railway. 449 policemen saw action, including 23 with police dogs, and 12 mounted police. The fans threw bottles, stones and rotten eggs at police. Some took off their shoes and used them as weapons. Others took off most of their clothing to dance and shout or climb stadium lamp-posts.'

... hier soll es billig Kleinholz geben?

'I heard you have a large supply of cheap firewood that's conveniently chopped?'

'We did a short tour of Germany sponsored by *Bravo* magazine, opening in Munster on 11th September, and virtually every gig was marked by rioting fans. We did two shows at the Ernst Merck Halle in Hamburg and played to 7,000 fans at each show and there were riots outside and police on horses continually charged fans, trying to disperse them. The police were incredibly brutal.

27th November 1965

The Beatles had famously played the Royal Command Performance in the presence of the Queen Mother and Princess Margaret on 4th November 1963. There was absolutely no chance of us ever being asked to do the same. On the day that this cartoon was published we were playing in America.

THE MILLSTONES: Good For The Image

I'VE HEARD IT SAID THAT WE'VE BEEN PICKED FOR THE 'ROYAL COMMAND'.

DO YOU THINK THERE'S ANY TRUTH IN IT?

NO! NOT REALLY I STARTED THE RUMOUR!

"We left Detroit and flew by charter plane to do a matinee show at the Hara Arena, Dayton, Ohio. In the evening we played The Gardens, Cincinnati, Ohio, for 2,500 fans. We had to temporarily abandon the show during the second song after fans rushed the stage."

'They had an unkempt, almost mangy look. The police struck me as being rougher than they need to be, and stopped the show during the 2nd number. One girl managed to reach the boys before she was bodily tackled by officers. One of the funnier moments at the show came just as it ended and the police were chasing the young girls who had broken through them to pursue the Stones through the rear-stage opening. One of the cops grabbed Brian Jones, a member of the Stones who has long blond hair and was wearing clothes that could be taken, at first glance, for a girl's costume. "What are you doing here?" growled the officer. Said Brian "I'm singing." It's even money as to which was the more surprised.'

The Cincinnati Post

Charlie   Bill   Brian   Mick   Keith

January 1966

These caricatures came from Germany.

May 1966

By the time this caricature appeared in the *New Musical Express* in May 1966 people were finding us slightly less weird than they had to begin with. It appeared a week after 'Paint It Black', our 10th UK single, was released. It got to No. 1 in both the UK and the US. According to Tom Jones, 'The thing I don't like about the Stones records is I can never understand any of the words. All I can understand in this is the title.' We recorded 'Paint It Black' in March at RCA in Los Angeles.

' While we were in the studio I started messing about on the Hammond doing a piss take of Eric Easton, who had once played professionally. Charlie immediately took up the rhythm and Brian played the melody line on sitar. I played normal bass at first and then on listening back to it, I suggested Hammond organ pedals. I lay on the floor under the organ, and played a second bass riff on the pedals with my fists, at double-time. '

28th October 1966

The *New Musical Express* featured a whole series of wonderful cartoons of bands and singers at this time. This was from their 28th October issue, four days after my 30th birthday. We had just finished a short tour with Ike and Tina Turner, and The Yardbirds with Jeff Beck and Jimmy Page, and our 11th UK single, 'Have You Seen Your Mother Baby, Standing In The Shadow' was in the charts. It was our first single for two and a half years not to have made the Top 3 in Britain. Besides us there's Andrew Oldham, our manager, sitting on top of his Rolls-Royce in the upper left of the cartoon.

The Redlands drug bust was our first grade A scandal – up to then, my peeing in a station forecourt and Keith being done for motoring offences was about as exciting as it got. It is the very stuff of which rock legend is made, a legend that could only have been bettered if George Harrison had been caught too! The story broke in the *News of the World* on 19th February, a week after the incident. In the report the paper failed to name names and stated that 'several stars, at least three of them nationally known names, were present at the party'.

> 'In the evening I went to the Olympic Studios, Barnes, where we cut 'Blues 1' (two versions). After the session, Keith, Mick, Marianne and a bunch of friends drove down to Redlands for the weekend.'

STEADman

Our visual reporter captures the dramatic moment when our gallant men in blue leap into the room and apprehend the miscreants.

14th April 1967

A month after Mick and Keith were charged with drug offences following their Redlands bust, and a month before they were to appear in court, this cartoon by the brilliant Osbert Lancaster appeared in the *Daily Express*. It shows how perceptions of us were changing: we were no longer just musicians, but something much more subversive. It was a foretaste of much of the humour surrounding the Stones to come.

On the day this appeared we were performing in Switzerland, having just played two shows behind the Iron Curtain in Poland.

POCKET CARTOON
by OSBERT LANCASTER

"If you ask me, it won't be the Daily Express or General de Gaulle who'll keep us out of Europe, but the Rolling Stones!"

© EXPRESS NEWSPAPERS

' In the morning, we checked out of the hotel (Warsaw), having found that our hotel bill came to EXACTLY the same amount as our proceeds from last night's concerts (!!!). '

While we were away in Europe on tour, Marianne Faithfull opened at London's Royal Court Theatre, playing Irina, one of the sisters in a new production of Chekhov's *Three Sisters*. This somehow encouraged people to think that Mick's acting ambitions stretched to Shakespeare! When Mick and Keith appeared in court on 10th May in Chichester there was a burst of creativity from the cartoonists.

"'Tis but a teenage jest, thou sayest? By the Bard, it had better be says I."

You can shee for yourshelf offisher—there'sh nothing illegal in our ashtrays.

29th June 1967

After their court appearance in May, Mick and Keith returned to Chichester to face a trial by jury.

Defending Mick was 44-year-old, future Attorney General, Michael Havers. For the prosecution Mr Malcolm Morris QC said, 'In a case of this sort it is right that I should say that you will decide this case entirely upon the evidence which you hear in this court. It may be that some of you have heard something about Mr Jagger, because he is somebody who may well be known to some of you.'

After the proceedings the jury took just six minutes to elect a foreman, and return their verdict. They found Mick guilty. Mr Havers asked for a certificate to appeal on a point of law. 'Yes, Mr Havers, and may I wish you luck,' said Judge Block.

"I'm his agent—I get twenty-five per cent of everything!"

SUNDAY EXTRA

"If only we could hire Judge Block to do ALL our publicity!"

'It's old Slash trying it on – in that gear he reckons he'll be out in 24 hours!'

Mick was sent to Lewes Jail for the night, returning to court in Chichester the following day for sentencing. He was taken to the remand wing and allowed to see his solicitors. They took him three books, one about Tibet and two on modern art. Mick asked for 40 Benson and Hedges cigarettes and was offered an evening meal before lights went out at 10 p.m. Judge Block sentenced Mick to three months, but two days later he and Keith, who had got 12 months, were out on appeal.

Pretty soon the press began to come out in support of Mick and Keith.

"We mustn't be prejudiced by their long hair."

HANDELSMAN

"Let us weigh without prejudice the defendants' insolence, flamboyance, wealth, youth, and the fact that we would love to put them behind bars."

'If British justice means anything, Mick Jagger was not on trial for being a Rolling Stone. He was not on trial for his hair, or his clothes, or his sounds. Or, in the eyes of the public, was he? Though the maximum penalty for possessing drugs, according to the Chairman, is ten years' jail, it is not usual for first offenders to be given as much as a prison sentence. First offenders are normally put on probation.'

John Heyes
The Evening News

45

1st November 1967

On 30 October it was Brian's turn to appear in court. Brian pleaded guilty to possessing a quantity of cannabis without authority, and permitting his premises to be used for the smoking of cannabis. He denied two charges of unlawfully possessing methedrine and cocaine; the prosecution accepted these pleas. James Comyn, defending Brian, pleaded with the court not to send him to jail. He said that while Brian had taken cannabis, he had had nothing to do with 'hard' drugs. But the judge jailed Brian for nine months for permitting his flat to be used for smoking cannabis. The following morning at the High Court, Brian's QC asked Mr Justice Donaldson to grant bail, pending an appeal against Brian's sentence. Having spent the previous 24 hours in Wormwood Scrubs Brian was freed on bail at 7 p.m.

PROTEST MARCH AGAINST ROLLING STONE'S SENTENCE

FRANKLIN

'The only protest heard when I got nine months was the wife screaming "Double it" . . .'

1968

Given Charlie's wonderfully expressive face it's surprising he wasn't caricatured more often in the early days. But then again it was usually Brian, and even more often Mick, who attracted the cartoonists. This is another by the great Jimmy Thomson from the *Melody Maker*. It was a great year for Charlie and his wife Shirley, as their daughter Seraphina was born on 18th March in Hove, Sussex. 1968 was almost like a year off for us as we only played one live show – the *New Musical Express* Poll Winners' concert at London's Wembley Arena, called the Empire Pool at the time.

1969

On Sunday 8th June Mick, Charlie and Keith spent the afternoon mixing at Olympic. I wasn't needed so I saved myself the five-hour round trip and stayed at home in Suffolk. During the afternoon they talked about Brian and what to do. On the spur of the moment they decided to drive down to Brian's house at Cotchford Farm, Sussex. The four of them talked for about an hour in what was a friendly discussion. Brian knew that he would probably be barred from America because of his drug offences. It was also questionable whether his body could stand up to the strain of a tour. There was another simple truth. Brian had moved away from us musically. He was contributing less and less in the studio and it was doubtful as to whether Brian could even contribute on stage anymore.

His Blues-based style was not where we were at any longer. We were a fully fledged rock band, and rock 'n' roll was not Brian. Mick, Keith and Charlie agreed that Brian should make a statement. Later in the evening it was officially announced that Brian had left the Stones. His place in the group would be taken by Mick Taylor.

On the evening of 2nd July Brian was found dead in the swimming pool at Cotchford Farm: he was just 27, and had lived the majority of his adult life in the spotlight. There have been too many conspiracy theories about Brian's death – now, as then, I think it was a dreadful accident.

Brian Jones

'*I no longer see eye to eye with the others over the discs we are cutting. We no longer communicate musically. The Stones' music is not to my taste anymore. I have a desire to play my own brand of music rather than that of others, no matter how much I appreciate their musical concepts. The only solution was to go our separate ways, but we shall still remain friends. I love those fellows.*'

Brian

5th July 1969

The week after Brian died we played our first gig with Mick Taylor on lead guitar in Hyde Park for a quarter of a million people. We went on stage at 5.25 p.m. Our reception was amazing. I can barely describe the feelings I had thinking how much Brian would have loved it – the hippy king with all his courtiers. Their warmth and affection seemed to come at us in waves. Mick had intended to wear a snakeskin suit designed by Ossie Clark, but at the last minute decided to wear 'the dress' as it was so hot. Mick then read from Percy Bysshe Shelley's poem 'Adonais'.

Life, like a dome of many-coloured glass,
Stains the white radiance of eternity,
Until death tramples it to fragments. – Die,
If thou wouldst be that which thou dost seek!

When Mick finished reading, Hyde Park erupted. We began with Johnny Winter's 'I'm Yours She's Mine', blasting the air with our music as 3,500 butterflies were released from cardboard boxes. People spoke of seeing Brian's ghost on stage with us, but in reality it was a large picture of Brian placed there.

6th July 1969

The day after the concert Mick and Marianne flew to Sydney via Los Angeles, where Mick was to begin filming *Ned Kelly*. Mick as Ned Kelly was not popular with some Australians. For weeks people had been protesting against 'a long-haired British pop star' playing their national hero, so when Mick and Marianne landed in Sydney, the waiting media found Mick dressed more like the Pied Piper than Ned Kelly, wearing a maroon maxi-length coat, black and white checked flared trousers, a white Isadora scarf, a straw hat, black field boots, and an Italian leather fringe purse over his shoulder. He wound up the waiting reporters by blowing them kisses.

MICK JAGGER AS NED KELLY IN FILM

FRANKLIN

© MIRRORPIX

'This is the scene where you smash twenty sheriffs to the ground with your handbag.'

'Huh! Those Australians. They really are dummies! But you can bet that there will probably be one or two people protesting when I get there – and I'll throw beer at them. They're so pathetic. When it comes to acting, they make out it's something special. It's not. It's just as natural as singing. You can either do it – or you can't.'

Mick
Daily Sketch

"I'd slip into yer armour smartly, Ned, mate."

6th December 1969

After Mick finished filming *Ned Kelly* we began a tour of the USA, playing 23 shows in 17 cities. It was on this tour that Sam Cutler, who acted as MC, began by introducing us as 'the greatest rock 'n' roll band in the world'. Towards the end of the tour we decided to play a free show in the San Francisco area. This became the infamous Altamont show at which rock 'n' roll's worst nightmares were realised. A crowd of around half a million showed up, a man high on LSD drowned in a river, two men sitting beside a road were badly injured by a hit and run driver, two babies were born, there was $400,000 worth of damage and Meredith Hunter was killed by the Hell's Angels who had been hired to act as concert stewards.

'Apart from all that, like how'd you enjoy the show?'

‘From the stage we trudged through thick mud, hardly able to see where we were going. We all piled into the helicopter with our ladies and friends, in all there were about twenty of us. There were really far too many for one helicopter – how the pilot managed to get airborne I'll never understand. We took off sideways, slowly gaining altitude, and we were flown back to San Francisco.’

4 BIRTHS, DEATHS, STABBINGS, AT 'STONES SHOW'

13th December 1969

'The Rolling Stones wreaked havoc, their defiance chilling authority, amusing us with their contempt for convention. In a way, the Stones have become an alter ego: a cathartic for our frustrations. At the same time they have hardened into possibly the best rock band in history.'

Kathy Orloff
Hollywood Reporter

'What can a Rolling Stone do at 40? It's the saddest thing in the world to contemplate a Rolling Stone in middle age.'

Douglas Hayward
Illustrated London News

Artwork by Brindley

The Stones with another hit album—Charlie Watts, Mick Taylor, Mick Jagger, Keith Richard, Bill Wyman.

'On Sunday 14th December, the day after this cartoon appeared, we played two shows at the Saville Theatre in the Strand, at 5 p.m. and 8.30 p.m. Ticket prices were 5/- to £1 and we were supported by Mighty Baby, Shakin' Stevens and the Sunsets, and David Berglass (a magician). Jeff Dexter was the compère. The gross was £1,585, and we received £310. Sir John Gielgud and Tony Richardson were among the audience. We played for just under an hour at each show.'

DJ John Peel said that Mick 'thinks he's leading some kind of workers' revolution', and asked 'how could he, living in a 40-roomed house somewhere and driving a Rolls-Royce?' John Peel's views were reinforced by Marianne Faithfull, who said that she and Mick 'went to the Earl of Warwick's house, which was beautiful. There were footmen behind every chair and I took a couple of mandies and passed out in the soup.' She went on to say that Mick was 'so humiliated by this – he had to carry me upstairs and put me to bed'.

FAN

"'Let's have some Stones on the record player' . . . they were your very words."

FAN

" You won't like this new Stones L.P, Dad . . . so I'll play it at 78 r.p.m. and get it over with twice as fast ! "

THE Seventies

Some have said that Altamont was the end of the sixties – the 'swinging sixties' that we had helped create – followed by the 'Summer of Love' in 1967 and the birth of the rock era. The decade finished with us releasing Let It Bleed, our first album with Mick Taylor, which heralded a new, tougher, sound for the band. In 1971 came Sticky Fingers and a year later Exile On Main St. – a period that gave the Rolling Stones musical immortality. Not that everyone agreed at the time. In January 1970 the *Melody Maker* had a suggestion: 'Let's hope in 1970 we see the break up of the Beatles and the Stones. Let's face it they've had a good innings and even they must admit their whole concept is now pure dullsville.'

Our answer in the late summer of 1970 was to mount our most ambitious European tour. We followed this with a mini-tour of Britain in March 1971, which was by way of a farewell to home as we were leaving to live in France to avoid a huge tax burden. Both our move to the south of France and Mick's wedding to Bianca gave the cartoonists a welcome new angle. Having bought a fifteenth-century moated manor house in Suffolk, it was very hard to spend time abroad and I tried to get back to the UK and my English home as often as the law allowed. Following the release of Exile on Main St., which was largely recorded at Keith's house in France, we toured North America and played to 750,000 people, which at that point made it the richest tour in history. In fact we could have played to millions; such was the demand for tickets.

In 1973 both Mick and Keith turned 30, and we had our third tour of Australasia, followed by our biggest ever tour of Europe to date – it was all very much business as usual. Our 14th British album (18th in the USA), Goats Head Soup, once again topped the charts in both countries, proving that we

© RECORD MIRROR

were as popular as ever. I began working on my solo album titled Monkey Grip; it was my very own piece of cockney rhyming slang! As a band we recorded 'It's Only Rock 'n' Roll', which was kept from the No. 1 spot by the Bay City Rollers – times were changing! They altered significantly in another way when Mick Taylor left us and Ronald David Wood joined. Woody brought a whole new dimension to the band, and not just from his playing. As Keith once said, 'Ronnie's a great mixture of talent and bullshit.' With Woody we did a 26-date tour of America, our first in three years – it seemed to take us into another dimension.

Black and Blue, our 1976 album, again failed to top the UK charts, but almost inevitably did the business in America. It preceded a European tour of 22 cities in nine countries, which gave the cartoonists a field day. We played a huge gig at Knebworth in August that was attended by around 200,000 people, and a couple of months later I turned 40. In 1977 we didn't tour, but released a live album and began work on the album that became Some Girls, which came out in June 1978. It went on to be a massive seller – our most successful US release since Sticky Fingers, helped by another big American tour in which we played smaller theatres, as well as the giant stadiums. It was our last tour of the decade, a period in which we had established ourselves as both a massive selling band and arguably the greatest live draw on the planet.

As 1979 came to an end I made a demo in my home studio in Vence, in the south of France. Called '(Si Si) Je Suis Un Rock Star', and sung in Franglais, it was an attempt at sending up my life as a Rolling Stone. Certainly if you'd have said to me in 1963 that I would still be playing with the Stones, or that we would even still exist, I would probably have laughed – but then again so would everybody else!

12th November 1970

The second official live album of our career, Get Your Yas Yas Out, came out in September 1970. As this cartoon attests, there had been and would be literally hundreds of bootlegs in circulation.

Blind Boy Fuller, real name Fulton Allen, born in North Carolina in 1908, was a Blues singer and it was he who first recorded a song called 'Get Your Yas Yas Out'. He was not blind as a child or teenager, but became partially blind in 1926 and fully blind when he was 20. He first recorded in July 1935 and shortly afterwards spent a short time in prison for shooting his wife.

Jo Bergman wrote to various French estate agents, saying she was looking for five houses of character in the south of France to rent for two years, in anticipation of our proposed move there in the spring.

19th December 1970

Newsweek said that American critics see rock sinking into a 'depression' from which new music is evolving. The magazine adds that Jagger may be joking now, 'but his move into the movies suggests that he recognises the limitations and dangers of being a superstar in rock'.

'In the end, I'm probably going to be like Cary Grant, with a lot of old ladies writing letters to me.'

Mick

'Better tell Geoffrey Rippon we've had the Common Market'

6th March 1971

When the news broke of our move to France it got us back into the mainstream press. This cartoon from the *Daily Mail* features the then Prime Minister Ted Heath.

17th March 1971

This appeared two days after we started a short 'Farewell to the UK' tour, which started in Newcastle and finished at London's Roundhouse 10 days later. Our move to France was prompted by the excessive tax demands on our earnings, and in particular those of Mick and Keith.

'Mon Dieu! Another trick to make us surrender to their Common Market terms!!'

14th May 1971

Mick and Bianca's wedding was scheduled for 4 p.m., but they delayed it about 30 minutes before the civil ceremony was supposed to take place, as Mick suddenly decided to take a late lunch and said, 'Bianca is still having her hair done.' It was further delayed when dozens of journalists and cameramen refused to clear the town hall room where the ceremony was to take place. They pointed out that civil wedding ceremonies were open to the public. Mick finally arrived with a trembling Bianca at 4.45 p.m. He asked photographers to take one last shot and leave them in peace.

'Ted, we must be 99 p.c. in if Mick Jagger is getting married in the Common Market.'

62

'Sorry we missed the quiet wedding bit, man, but this is more like our scene.'

At 4.55 p.m. Mick was married to Bianca Perez Morena de Macias. Mayor Marius Astezan conducted the ceremony. Keith was Best Man, and Patrick Lichfield gave Bianca away. The witnesses were Natalie Delon, Roger Vadim, Keith and Francois Gouglietto. Among the other people who attended, were Mick's parents and Anita. Having made the entry in the register, they drove in Mick's white Bentley to the blessing at the seventeenth-century Catholic Chapel of St Anne, on a hilltop overlooking St Tropez bay. As the couple exchanged rings, a classical wedding march was played, and then, at the request of the bride, a medley of themes from the film *Love Story*. After the ceremony, they returned to the Hotel Byblos.

'Keith Richard turned up in black braided tights and green combat jacket – and was promptly refused admission.'

John Ellison
Daily Express

MICK JAGGER MARRIES IN SECRET

FULL REPORT AND PICTURES

Bany Gumbut

Mini-Trog

THE JAGGER WEDDING

'They make a lovely couple.'

' Charlie and Shirley arrived at our house, and we went with them, and Mick Taylor and Rose, to the Hotel Byblos in St Tropez, and met up with everybody. At 10 p.m. we attended the wedding reception at the little theatre alongside the Café des Arts, in St Tropez. Bianca had changed into a small open bolero top, revealing her breasts to everyone. There were about 500 fans outside. Mick had chartered a Dan Air Comet airliner to bring friends from London to attend the wedding reception. '

COOKSON.

"I hope our doubles in St. Tropez are coping with all the razzamatazz!"

The debate about whether or not Britain should be allowed to join the Common Market seemed to go on forever – longer even than the coverage of Mick and Bianca's wedding! In showing Prime Minister Edward Heath as a French cleric and Georges Pompidou's eyebrows the cartoonists combined their love of political targets with their favourite celebrity.

"But, my dear, one sweet girl has already married a hairy man in Europe—why shouldn't you?"

Cummings

'Everything was going fine, Ted, until I came to the bit about Mick Jagger and the Rolling Stones being our contribution to the E.E.C. budget'

September 1971

This cartoon was prompted by the news that we had severed our connections with Allen Klein and had begun legal proceedings to try to get back what we felt was rightfully ours. Seated at the desk is Leslie Perrin, our long-time publicist. It was Leslie who often bore the brunt of the attacks upon us but he was well up to the task. Leslie had been in PR for many, many years and worked with just about everyone from Frank Sinatra and Nat King Cole to Cliff Richard and the Shadows.

29th November 1971

On Monday 29th November Mick, Bianca and Jade, Keith, Anita and Marlon, Mick Taylor, Rose and Chloe, Jimmy Miller and Andy Johns all flew from Nice to Paris, then from Paris to London. But on boarding a plane to Los Angeles, there was an incident.

'Just because it sounds extra noisy, that doesn't mean Mick Jagger is aboard'

'An investigation was ordered after reports from Pan American staff at Heathrow about incidents aboard the plane. Mick Jagger flew in aboard the airliner from Paris with his wife and 7 travelling-companions. The airliner had been held up by bad weather and the transit time at Heathrow had to be cut short. Mr. Jagger and his friends were on their way from a jumbo jet pier to the airline's VIP suite when it was realised that by the time they got there it would be time to re-board the aircraft. The party were taken back and it was then that the trouble started. According to one official at Heathrow there was a queue of passengers to board the flight but the Jagger party ignored it. The group then went aboard and took seats in the 1st class compartment. They had 1st class tickets, but took the wrong seats. Mr. Jagger and his friends were asked to move but they refused and according to one airline official they said: "We will sit where we like." Pan-American officially confirmed a complaint of foul language. After the captain said that he would not fly the airliner unless Mr. Jagger and his friends sat in the proper seats and behaved themselves, they agreed to do this.'

Evening News

'The story is a load of nonsense. They've made a mountain out of a molehill really. Some people had not turned up to take their seats next to us and we wanted to put one of the children in an empty seat. A receptionist came onto the plane and told us we couldn't use the seat. She was very rude. There was no need to be silly about seating. There was plenty of room and it was not as if we were on a school outing. But she said if we didn't take the child off the seat we couldn't go at all. I said "don't be silly" and she said "I'll see that you don't fly Pan Am again." Then she went and spoke to another hostess who said "They should put them all out at 30,000 feet."'

Mick

" Forget the stewardess who said she'd like to drop you off at 30,000ft., Mick—Dad here says he'd make it 60,000."

May 1972

Our album Exile on Main St. came out in Britain at the end of May. In an interview to promote it Mick spoke about some of our future plans.

'Next year, we are going to do a very different kind of tour. We will go with The Who, take our own tent, which will hold about 10,000, and we will play each town for five days. We will have our own train, too. The whole thing will be a sort of rock 'n' roll carnival with games, and circus acts, and things like that. We will be making a film of it, too. And it should be a hell of a film. I don't like the idea of middle-aged pop stars. Elvis looks pretty fat these days, but then he is ten years older than me. I would not like to go on that long. I suppose the band could go on playing for ever. I mean, the others are pretty old now. Just look at them.'

© MIRRORPIX

JAGGER—the bison.

'Mick Jagger is a North American bison. Not only is the physical likeness quite striking, but also their mating calls are practically identical. It could also explain all that hair.'

Christopher Ward
Daily Mirror

Jean Acko '72

'If Jesus Christ came to town, he couldn't sell more tickets. The Stones can get away with whatever they want. They're universals. They're Gods, they ain't even immortals anymore. They're whites makin' black music. Everybody black digs the Stones. Everybody white. And they even got the Chinese and the Mexicans, too. I can't play enough Stones. My switchboard lights up whenever a cut from the new album goes on.'

Wolfman Jack
Rolling Stone *magazine*

Somebody painted and gave me this vest on the tour; I wore it a lot!

18th July 1972

'What made you nostalgic, Simon? A minister resigning or the arrest of Mick Jagger?'

'We went to Montreal airport to fly to Boston. The Charter plane made two attempts to take off, breaking each time, and going back. Then we had a two-hour wait, while they fixed the fault. We then flew for Boston, but after 30 minutes we heard that the airport was closed down with fog. We were diverted to Bedford (16 miles from Boston), and then diverted again to Green Airport, Warwick, Rhode Island, where we finally landed. We went through customs, and were getting ready to leave, when a photographer [Andy Dickerman for the Providence Journal-Bulletin] arrived in the customs area, and caused a big scene trying to take photos of us. Our security people tried to stop him, and Keith eventually hit him lightly around the legs with his belt. At around 8 p.m., the local police arrived and took his side against us. Mick, Keith, Marshall Chess, Robert Frank and Stan Moore were all arrested, and taken to a local jail. Mick was charged with obstructing a police officer, while Keith was booked on a charge of simple assault. Robert Frank and Marshall Chess were charged with obstructing a policeman, and Stanley Moore was charged with simple assault. The photographer was taken to a Providence hospital with a wrenched arm and a shoulder injury. Police said he had also been hit in the side with a belt. Mick, Keith and the others pleaded not guilty at a special session of Rhode Island District Court.

August 1972

Mick had just turned 29.

'When I'm 33, I quit. That's the time when a man has to do something else. I can't say what it will definitely be. It's still in the back of my head – but it won't be in show business. I don't want to be a rock 'n' roll singer all my life. I couldn't bear to end up as an Elvis Presley and sing in Las Vegas with all those housewives and old ladies coming in with their handbags. It's really sick. Elvis probably digs it. That's his good fortune if that's the way he wants it. Not me. Millionaire? Nowhere near it. Half my money has been stolen. I don't have any money. I never did. I only have enough to exist on.'

Mick
Daily Mirror

STONES UNABLE TO PLAY LINCOLN BECAUSE OF TAX REGULATIONS

"IS IT ALL RIGHT IF I SING IN THE BATH?"

While no band likes to be bootlegged I can't help admiring this cover artwork of a bootleg of our 1972 tour.

February 1973

You'll notice that Keith is missing. The original was hanging in Sticky Fingers, my London restaurant, from where it was stolen!

The third tour down under included shows in Hawaii and was originally scheduled to include five shows at the Budoken in Tokyo and two shows in Hong Kong, but these were cancelled. It was far from the best tour of our career. The playing was sloppy on some gigs and we also had too many niggling technical problems.

In the early days a Coke or a beer would have done the trick. By now everyone had his own favourite tipple on tap.

Everyone: Dom Perignon, Moët & Chandon, Krug, beer; Mick: Jack Daniel's Black, beer, Wild Turkey; Keith: Cuevaro Gold Tequila, orange juice, grenadine; Bill: vodka, 7 Up, lemonade; Charlie: everything; Mick T: Courvoisier cognac, Bourbon and Coke, Kahlua; Bobby Keys: Jack Daniel's Black; Jim Price: Jack Daniel's Black; Nicky Hopkins: Johnnie Walker and Coke.

"On Thursday 8th February, we arrived in Sydney in pouring rain, and eight customs men gave us a heavy two-hour going-over. We checked into the Kingsgate Hotel, in King's Cross, under new pseudonyms of famous racing cyclists: Mick (H. Porter), Keith (L. West), me (T. Simpson), Charlie (E. Merckx), Mick Taylor (P. Baynton), Bobby (B. Hoban), Jim (S. Lovatt), Nicky (C. Lewis), and Marshall (F. Bracke). We also used famous cricketers' names: Mick (W.G. Grace), Keith (Freddie Truman), Charlie (Trevor Bailey), me (Len Hutton), Mick Taylor (Peter May), Bobby Keys (Jack Hobbs), Jim Price (Herbert Sutcliffe), Nicky Hopkins (Tony Lock). Others were: Peter Rudge (Ted Heath), and Alan Dunn (Harold Wilson)."

28th February 1973

This cartoon appeared in the Australian *Daily Mirror* on the day after we finished our Australian tour. The night before we had played the racetrack in Sydney.

'The Stones arrived in their carriage drawn by white horses. The crowd roared when the floodlights lit up the Stones riding down the track. 25,000 clapped, cheered and sang along with the Stones.'

Daily Telegraph
Australia

'Keith Richard changed his axe after every number – but, as far as I could hear, it didn't help his playing any. Mick Taylor played some beautiful slide licks. Mick Jagger was his effervescent self.'

John Robinson
Music Maker

'A decade of social revolution has slipped across the Western hemisphere while the Stones grind inexorably on. There'll probably come a day when their records no longer get into the charts automatically, and they won't be able to sell out auditoriums. They'll be another piece of nostalgia from the mid-seventies. That's more like life. It's also a kind of death in itself, a decay that eats away at the heart of pop culture with frightening voracity. This tour represents more comprehensively than the American one, however, how much longer they're all able to go into the Seventies.'

Michael Watts
Melody Maker

Beginning in Vienna, our European tour of 1973 was the biggest tour of Europe we had undertaken. We played 20 cities in eight countries. It was also pretty lucrative, as we made a profit of over £250,000.

This cartoon from France has the headline, above my head, 'The Rolling Stones back in Europe in the autumn' with the other caption saying 'He has dared to sell us to this sordid rock trafficker.' No, I don't get it either!

November 1973

'We took Ron [Wood] along because, just as we were about to leave, Mick [Taylor] had to be treated for sinusitis.'

Mick

Midway through November we went to Munich to record at the Musicland Studios with Andy Johns. Mick Taylor went down with a 'mystery' illness, and didn't arrive in Munich, so Ron Wood came along and played on one of the tracks. We finished and flew back to London on 25th November.

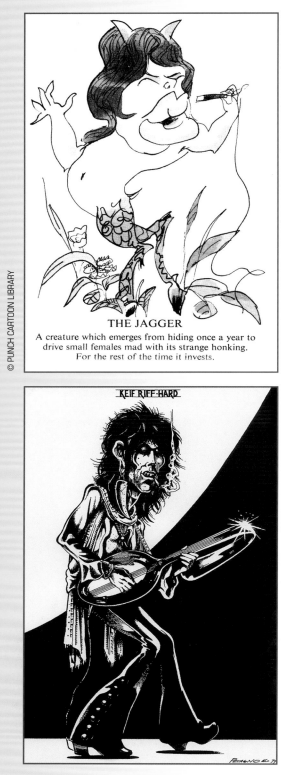

THE JAGGER

A creature which emerges from hiding once a year to
drive small females mad with its strange honking.
For the rest of the time it invests.

Ronnie and Keith's New Barbarian's band with Ian McLagan, Willie Weeks and Andy Newmark played the Gaumont State Theatre in Kilburn, London NW6. They were supported by Chilli Willi and The Red Hot Peppers, and Rod Stewart made a guest appearance.

'Rod Stewart appears from the left of the stage and vamps up James Rae's "If You Gotta Make A Fool of Somebody" with Wood and Keith, straight through "Mystifies Me" and finishes off with a dynamic rocker which no one bothers to introduce the title of. Keith Richard lurches over to the electric piano which he will go on to play quite agreeably on one of his songs called "Act Together", a reflective love ballad for all intents and purposes.'

Nick Kent
New Musical Express

July 1975

These two caricatures of Mick appeared in Britain while we were in the middle of a massive US tour, in which we played to over a million people at 45 shows in 26 cities. The cartoon on the right appeared in the *Melody Maker* on 19th July. The following day we played Hughes Stadium, Fort Collins, Colorado. We went on stage, where we were joined by Elton John, who was supposed to play two or three songs with us. He ended up playing through the whole show.

'The technical term is "outstaying your welcome": Elton John joined the Stones onstage in Denver – and three-quarters of an hour later he was still there, and Certain People (like Mick, Keef, Honest Ron, Billy, Bill, Charlie et al.) were Not Smiling; after the show Elt hosted a barbecue in the Stones' honour at Caribou Ranch, and the guests of honour didn't show.'

New Musical Express

> *Al Kooper and his girlfriend, and Keith Moon and Annette Walter-Lax, visited, and invited us to Peter Sellers' birthday party tonight. It was held at Peter's house. Other guests included: Hugh Hefner, Peter Cook, Marty Feldman, Henry Mancini and Tony Curtis. There was a stage set up, and I ended up having a jam with Ronnie Wood, Keith Moon, Nigel Olsson, Joe Cocker, Danny Kortchmar, Jesse Ed Davis, David Bowie, Steve Madeo and Bobby Keys. It was hopeless, and we couldn't get one song together between us.*

2nd September 1975

Mick gave an interview to *Creem* magazine, and, as the cartoon implies, talked at length about his own career and that of the band. On the day it came out I was in Los Angeles recording for my solo album and on the day that *Creem* was issued I went to a party at Peter Sellers' house.

25th October 1975

This cartoon appeared the day after my 39th birthday. Fortunately the same holds true today!

'Midnight. And things were fast taking shape. The vast stage cost £150,000. A team of 14 have spent virtually the entire month in a Shepperton studio practising constructing it in the swiftest possible time. They have it down to eight hours. A bank of 300 lights, weighing an incredible 16 tons & suspended 30ft above the stage, & a mirror, all of 25ft long by 6ft was turned at an angle towards the stage hovering some 20ft away. Someone asked what on earth will emerge from 30ft of black rubber piping which at the moment was flopping all over the stage. Jagger & Wyman turned up. Jagger inspected the lights & positioning of a catwalk down from the stage along which he will jiggle. The whole place had now taken on an intense deep red glow & at 1.30 a.m. it was like a scene from Quatermass. At 2.15 the first sounds were heard – Billy Preston's keyboard. Then a drum roll which is the opening of 'Honky Tonk Woman'. But Mick was not concerned about sounds tonight. Jagger decided to call it a day. It was 3 a.m.'

Garth Pearce
Daily Express

"Fortunately, their audience has grown up with them"

84

1976

The cover of a French book that
came out in 1976.

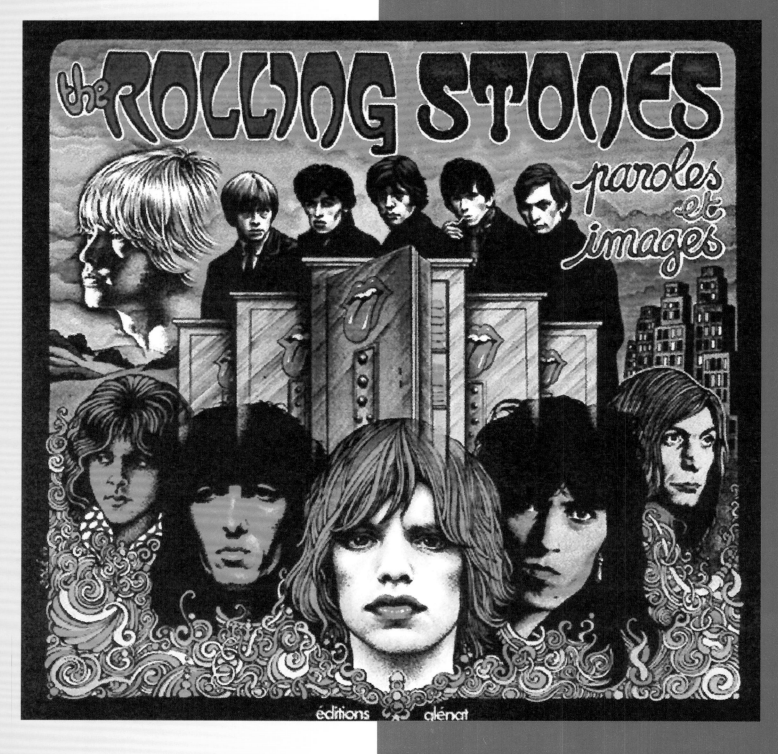

"On Monday 26th April, we flew to Frankfurt. On arrival I found that the suitcase containing all my stage clothes was missing. I checked into the Park Hotel as Robin Day. The rest of the band were also under pseudonyms. Ronnie ('Patrick Moore'), Mick ('Arthur Ashe'), Billy Preston ('James Burke'), Charlie ('Peter West'), Keith ('Percy Thrower')."

Two days later we started a European tour that took in 22 cities in nine countries, at which we played 41 shows.

23rd and 25th May 1976

The cartoon to the right appeared in the *Sunday Times* on the day of our third show at Earl's Court.

The cartoon below was featured in *The Times* and appeared on the morning of our fourth Earl's Court show.

'I'm having to chaperone Mummy to the Stones concert...'

© MARC

5th June 1976

The *Melody Maker* cartoon on the right was featured in the issue dated 5th June, which is when we played Aux Abattoires, in Paris.

Heath-note

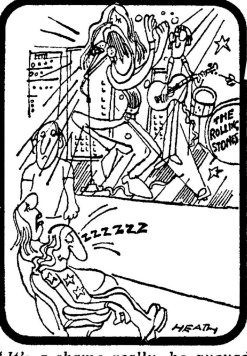

" It's a shame really, he queued up all night."

© THE SUNDAY TIMES/NI SYNDICATION

We went to the venue, and I played table tennis backstage. Princess Margaret arrived to meet us, and we were expected to line up to meet her. Unfortunately, when she got there I was in the toilet, but I got out in time to be introduced. Yehudi Menuhin was there to see the show – he hated it!

We went to the venue. We were supported by The Meters and John Miles. We went onstage and did a very good show. The audience was one of the best on the tour so far. The show was recorded live, and video was shot. While we changed backstage after the show, a guy burst in brandishing a pistol, which caused some excitement, before he was caught. Everyone was remarkably calm during this incident.

MICK, JAGGER'S CHARISMA

Kipper Williams

We played the Show: Olympiahalle, Munich. We went onstage at 8 p.m. and did a great show to quite a good audience. Later, back at the hotel, we went to Keith's room and heard a cassette of a rough mix of the third Paris show, which was mostly good.

July 1976

This came from the July issue of *Rolling Stones 76* magazine and was inspired by our career as criminals!

275119 WYMAN

114109 RICHARD

105293 JAGGER

246427 WATTS

173426 JONES

437104 TAYLOR

6th August 1976

Princess Margaret coming to see our shows prompted this cartoon (right), which was prophetic by 25 years or so!

"Well, fans—we haven't made the Honours List so far —but after this . . ."

© MIRRORPIX

We stayed at Hugh Hefner's Playboy Mansion for four days during our 1972 tour of the USA. A lack of space prevents me from giving you any more details! On our 1975 American tour we flew everywhere on our own chartered aircraft – the Starship – which was a converted Boeing 707.

'I'd better warn the passengers, Chief. We seem to have inadvertently violated Hugh Hefner's air space.'

30th November 1976

Mick and Bianca were on holiday in Mustique the day this cartoon appeared in the *Daily Express*. Two days earlier they had been to Colin Tennant's 50th birthday party, where Princess Margaret was among the guests.

© EXPRESS NEWSPAPERS

A week earlier the Sun *had said:*

'Tax exile Mick Jagger and his wife Bianca are coming back to live in London. "The sooner the better," says Mick. The 33-year-old singer is tired of being a "rolling stone" – constantly moving from one rented house to another in America and the south of France. Mick said: "Never mind the taxes. I have been away too long and London is the only real place to live." When they return in a week they plan to start house hunting. As a top taxpayer Mick will have to hand over 83p in the £ on earnings over £20,000 net a year.'

'Mick Jagger denied that he is having an affair with trendy Margaret Trudeau, wife of the Canadian Premier. She was reported to have run off with Jagger to New York after staying in the same hotel as the Stones in Toronto. And her husband was alleged to be so angry that he wanted her put on a plane and escorted back to Canada by Government agents. He was said to be "going up the wall" in his attempt to persuade his wife to return before the scandal ruined him politically. But Jagger said: "This is ridiculous. I only just met the girl at the weekend and I have no idea where she is now. She's a very likeable person, but there's no romantic attachment at all." A spokesman for the Rolling Stones continued to deny vehemently that she was with either Jagger or Wood. "In fact, I have just left Mick, who is with Bianca in their town house," claimed the group's spokesman, Paul Wasserman.'

Mark Dowdney
Daily Mirror

'She obviously prefers older men.'

10th March 1977

Two years after Margaret Thatcher was elected Conservative Party leader, this archetypal Osbert Lancaster cartoon appeared in the *Daily Express*. We were in Canada at the time, with Keith about to face a Canadian court on drugs charges. Given that Mrs Thatcher's favourite record was 'Telstar' by the Tornadoes, it's none too surprising she didn't like us!

19th March 1977

Some of what was behind this cartoon was down to the fact that we had spent some time in Toronto with Margaret Trudeau, the soon-to-be ex-wife of the Canadian Prime Minister. As she explained to the *Daily Express*, 'Pierre [Trudeau] & I reached our decision to part on our sixth wedding anniversary. I was packing my cases to leave for New York when a call came from a friend, Penny Royce, in Toronto. "How about dinner with the Rolling Stones?" she suggested, half joking. "Why not?" I replied a little bitterly. "I'm free. I've just left Pierre." When I reached the airport that Friday I found that Penny had checked me into the Harbor Castle Hotel, because, as she explained in the car on our way into town, the Stones were staying there & we could sneak more discreetly into their suite for the dinner she had arranged. My first meeting with the Rolling Stones was over drinks. Mick Jagger was polite & charming. We drank wine. There were no drugs about.'

January 1978

Either Mick or the *Daily Mail* got it wrong in saying that Hal Ashby directed *Rocky*, because it was in fact John G. Avildsen. Hal did later work with us, directing *Let's Spend The Night Together* in 1983, and back in 1978 he was just about to start filming *Being There* with Peter Sellers.

'On Sunday 22nd January, at 3.30 a.m. I went to a recording session at the Pathe Marconi Studios in Boulogne with engineer Chris Kimsey – Mick said he was sick, and Ronnie and Keith didn't come. Only Charlie and I were there – I did bass o/dubs until 6 a.m. Keith arrived at 7 a.m. I left at 8 a.m. Mick left and flew to New York. He returned next day.'

NEWS

BIANCA JAGGER STAYED IN LAST NIGHT AND WASHED HER HAIR

HEATH

'With the stirring promise that she will never agree to a divorce, Bianca Jagger flew from California to New York for a meeting with the errant Mick after his holiday with Texan model Jerry Hall. Mick left his Paris pied-à-terre for talks in America about a television special which is being planned around his multifarious talents. Provisionally titled Mick, the show is intended to launch him on the next stage of his career. As a keen fan of Rocky, Mick would like Hal Ashby, who directed the Oscar-winning movie, to take charge of his project and is also deep in discussion concerning national networking of the programme.'

Daily Mail

25th June 1978

On the day this brilliant Gerald Scarfe cartoon appeared in the *Sunday Times* we were in the middle of a US tour. The following day we played the Coliseum, Greensboro, North Carolina.

Gerald Scarfe

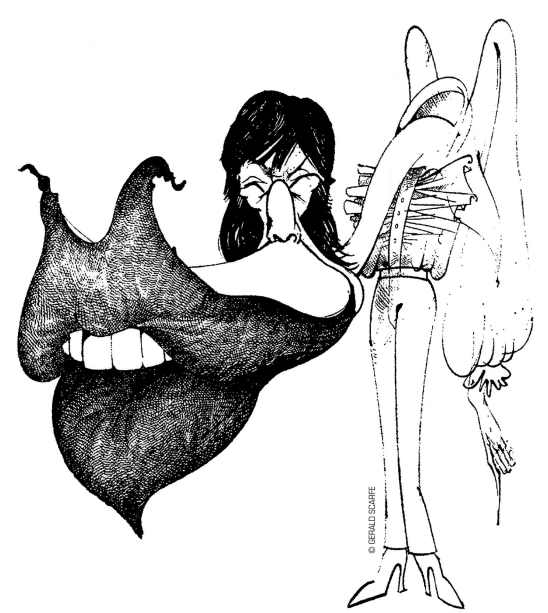

'For the last 14 years Mick Jagger has been singing rock 'n' roll for the Rolling Stones. Mick Jagger is a camping, vamping James Dean up top and down below gyrating androgyny outfitted in leather pants whose elastic grabs his groin with obscenely bulging effect; a prancing, high-stepping leprechaun; a vulgar fellow given to fondling himself in public; the greatest rock 'n' roll singer going. Eighteen songs and a 90-minute performance did nothing to dispel the myth perpetuated over a generation and a half that their Satanic Majesties can whip up a crowd like nobody else going.'

David Newton
Greensboro
Daily News

"On Monday 10th July, we played the Civic Centre, St Paul, Minnesota, at 7.30 p.m. Our support act was Peter Tosh. Mick sang 'Don't Look Back' with him. We went onstage and did a very good show to a great audience of 17,500 fans. At the end of the show I ran offstage the wrong way and fell through the curtain at the back of the stage, and landed on the concrete 7ft below. I hit my head and cut it a bit, hit my shoulder, arm, wrist and hand, and was knocked out. I was taken to the local emergency hospital and admitted for the night. Astrid and Jim Callaghan came with me, and Jim stayed the night. Mick phoned, and I also spoke to Keith and they sent letters to me. They did X-rays everywhere and checked me out. I was finally able to get off to sleep at about 4.45 a.m."

15 July 1978

Five days before this cartoon appeared it was me who was in the wars. We were in the middle of a US tour when I chipped the knuckle-bone of the middle finger of my left hand. It left me with a badly swollen hand and I had to play like that for the next three weeks, until the end of the tour.

May 1979

On Wednesday 2nd May, Bianca Jagger celebrated her 34th birthday. The following day Mick was in the High Court for the latest in their divorce proceedings.

'Mick Jagger seemed surprised to see Hollywood lawyer Marvin Mitchelson arrive for the private hearing. Mitchelson is on record as saying that Jagger is "a penny-pinching scrooge". He and the Rolling Stone have crossed swords before. In January Mitchelson won a paternity suit against him on behalf of American singer Marsha Hunt. Jagger flew in for the hearing from his current home in New York, where his regular companion is model Jerry Hall. She has been named by Bianca as the 'other woman'. Bianca is claiming half of the singer's £12,500,000 fortune, plus £5,000 for herself and £2,000 a month for their seven-year-old daughter Jade.'

Thomson Prentice
Daily Mail

"Your wife called while you were out, Mr Jagger."

December 1979

By the time this cartoon appeared in the *Toronto Globe* on 1st December 1979 work on our new album had ground to a halt. About a week or so later Mick and Keith continued to work on the album again, at Electric Lady Studios, New York. I was at home in Vence and on Wednesday 19th December I did a demo session at the house and wrote '(Si Si) Je Suis Un Rock Star' overnight.

' Took her to a disco in Battersea
I asked her to dance and then she danced with me.
And then I took a chance, come home with me today,
I live in France, we can get there BEA

Je suis un Rock Star, J'avais un residence.
Je Habite la a la south of France
Voulez vous partir with me
And come and restez la with me in Vence '

'NOW, FOLKS, WE TURN FROM SKATING TO MATING . . .'

THE Eighties

The decade began with something of a fanfare as 'Emotional Rescue' went to No. 1 in both America and Britain. The album had taken such a long time to get together and so it was surprising when it stayed at No. 1 in the USA for seven weeks – longer than any other in our 16-year history. However, from that point things went pretty much downhill. We were not really working as a band, and we all spent time on our own projects. In early 1981 we released Sucking in the Seventies, a compilation of various old tracks. Probably as a reflection of the way things were for us, it became our first 'official' album not to chart in the UK. A few months after the album came out my solo single '(Si Si) Je Suis Un Rock Star' made the UK charts and became a sizeable hit in many countries. We found it difficult to agree on anything, although we finally decided that we should tour after finishing work on another album. Tattoo You was completed in New York and like its predecessor was made up of old tracks – many that didn't make it onto Emotional Rescue.

Our US tour lasted from late September to mid-December 1981. We played to over 2 million people at 50 shows in 28 cities in 20 states. Put into perspective, we played to more people at many individual dates on this tour than on both our first US tours put together! Almost six months later we started a European tour, which like the American tour was our biggest to date. It had been six years since we had toured the UK and Europe and the demand for tickets was enormous. We played 25 gigs in 22 cities in 10 countries to almost 1.7 million people, almost three times as many as we had in 1976. It was yet another opportunity to portray us in cartoons – could we really be that old and still performing? Following this tour the band went into what can only be termed a fallow period. A live album came out, which was followed by Undercover in November 1983; it was less of a success than many previous albums. Another greatest hits compilation, Rewind, came out in the summer of 1984, and it struggled to No. 86 in America and No. 23 in Britain. This was also a quiet time for the cartoonists – only Mick's 40th birthday and my relationship with Mandy Smith offered them much in the way of sustenance. Our album recorded over the first six months of 1985 hit the stores in March 1986. Dirty Work was non-vintage Stones and its success in America was largely as a result of our cover version of Bob and Earl's 1963 hit, 'Harlem Shuffle', doing so well on the Hot 100. We dedicated Dirty Work to our old mate Ian Stewart, who had been with the band since the beginning and who had tragically died in December 1985.

Throughout 1987 and 1988 we were mostly distant from each other, but we did finally get back to recording in early 1989. I married Mandy, which got everyone's attention once again. Our tour, which began in August 1989, was named after our album Steel Wheels, released in September. So by the end of the decade we were back doing what we did best – playing live.

21st August 1980

Emotional Rescue became our first album since 1973's Goats Head Soup to top the album chart in both Britain and America, despite the arguments that had gone on between Mick and Keith. What was perhaps most surprising was the fact that it topped the US album chart for seven weeks, longer than any other Stones album at that time.

© RECORD WORLD

When this cartoon about Mick and Bianca appeared in the *Melody Maker* I was busy in the studio working on the soundtrack material I had composed for the film *Green Ice*.

A SMILE, a song and a million quid! That's the figure which Bianca Jagger is understood to have settled for in her divorce from Mick Jagger.

The actual figure may never be known, but the figure one, followed by six zeroes, is whispered. Bianca married Mick in 1971 at St Tropez.

26th September 1981

Our US tour opened at JFK Stadium in Philadelphia on 25th September.

> *At 2.15 p.m. everyone left, and we went down and got into our van (Mick, Charlie and I). Jerry was here from yesterday, and Jade had arrived. We drove to the venues and had no problems.. We met up backstage with Jane Rose, Bill Graham, George Thorogood and friends. Vitas Gerulaitis promised to get me tennis clothes in New York, and bring McEnroe to meet us. We finally went onstage at 4 p.m., and played for two hours. The sound today was really good, and I had a great show. The weather was hot and sunny again, and we had another wonderful crowd of 90,000.*

Doghouse Riley

'I can't go on pretending to be eighteen much longer.'

Mick at the start of the tour

FLYING WITH MICK

© SENTINEL STAR

23rd October 1981

This caricature appeared in Orlando's *Sentinel Star* the day before we played two days at the city's Tangerine Bowl – the first of which was my 45th birthday.

The running order was: Henry Paul Band, Van Halen, and then we went onstage at 2.30 p.m. and played to 60,000 for two hours, in a very hot and humid atmosphere. There were many banners in the crowd with birthday wishes. I had my new speaker system here, and it sounded great for a change. I wore my yellow suit. Then a plane started flying around with 'Happy Birthday Bill', from Freddie and friends. After the introductions, Mick got the crowd to sing 'Happy Birthday', which was really something. We had a great show.

MICK TAYLOR

BRIAN JONES

RON WOOD

109

June 1982

We began a tour of the UK and Europe on 26th May at Aberdeen's Capitol Theatre. It was the opportunity for the cartoonists to ply their trade. It was our first European tour in six years and we played to over 1.6 million people at 35 gigs in 23 cities and 10 countries.

© THE SUN/NI SYNDICATION

"Whatever happened to the Mick Jagger look-alike I married in 1965?"

Memo From Jagger

Illustration: Jill Mumford

'We played a show at the Hippodrome D'Auteuil, Paris. There were many guests here, including Jerry Hall and her Bianca-looking friend, Patti Hansen, Jo, Johnny Piggozi, Shirley Watts, Cynthia Stewart and James Karnbach. We went onstage from 5.15 p.m. to 7.30 p.m. and played our usual set – it rained on and off a little, but not as bad as it could have (we had torrential downpours and lightning at the hotel earlier). The crowd here seemed more like 80,000 to me. The sound wasn't too good and audience were reasonably quiet. We left and returned to the hotel with friends, then Spiros Niarchos arrived. At 11 p.m. we all went to dinner at the Elysée Matignon. Bobby Keyes also came. We were later joined by Alan Edwards. We had good food, then Serge Gainsborough joined us and began mixing cocktails from Tequila and pink champagne. We went downstairs and joined Mick and Jerry, and Roman Polanski was there too. We left at 4.30 a.m. and returned to the hotel. I had drinks in reception with Mick McKenna and friends for an hour or so, then got back to my room. I got off to sleep at 6.30 a.m.'

'At 5 p.m. I flew with Bobby Keys and Gene Barge by helicopter from Battersea to Wembley in about 10 minutes, avoiding 1½ hours in the car. The running order was: Black Uhuru (4 p.m.), J. Geils Band (5 p.m.), and the Stones (6.30 p.m.). Backstage I played table tennis with John McEnroe and lost a very close game. He refused to play me again. We went onstage and had a very good concert, with good weather and good sound. I was very pleased with our performance.'

This cartoon appeared in the *Sun* on the first of two shows we played at Wembley Stadium. At lunchtime before the show I went to a music charity lunch and among those I sat and chatted with were George Best and Dame Margot Fonteyn — both of whom shared the same talents of grace, balance and skill.

JAGGER DRESSING ROOM

BOWi

"Mick, there's a new tube of lipstick for you!"

© THE SUN/NI SYNDICATION

111

3rd July 1982

The *Daily Mirror* ran this caricature the day we played Vienna.

'At 4 p.m. we left and drove by van to the venue with Bob Bender and Marlon. When we arrived at the stadium the driver went a bit mad with kids running all over the place. He sped up and hit a guy, who ran across the road without looking. The guy looked pretty bad in the road, and we were there 20 minutes. The windscreen was smashed in, and the driver was out of his head with shock. Bender was trying to get the police to take us into the venue. Then ambulances arrived to look after the guy. The vans bringing Keith, Woody, Charlie, and entourage arrived, and we switched to theirs and got into the venue. We heard later that he had a fractured skull, then later still that he wasn't too bad.'

This appeared in *Rolling Stone* two days before we played Slane Castle in Dublin, the penultimate date on our European tour.

'At 2 p.m. Keith arrived and talked to me about the donations to the bomb victims of the IRA in London last week, and the show, and promptly fell asleep on our sofa. At 2.45 p.m. Patti came to our room and got Keith up, and back to his room to get ready for the show. At 3 p.m. we left by van with Stu, Chuck, and Gene Barge, and drove to the heliport. At 3.30 p.m. we left by helicopter and flew 15 minutes to Slane Castle. Guests backstage included Sabrina, Miranda and Hugo Guinness, and Sara Marks. We went on stage at 6.15 p.m. and did our usual two-hour set. The crowd were great and the show was good too.'

This cartoon strip about our 1982 European tour came from Finland. I have no idea what it says but I think it captures the essence of those days very well.

This is what *Sounds*, the British weekly music paper, had to say about one of our two Wembley shows:

'In essence the Stones are still regurgitating jivin' rhythms an' blues or Motown marvelling through the night. But them Telecasters janglin' shambolically yet astoundingly hearty & tuneful are just a joy to hear. Keith especially seems to handle his guitars with carefree brashness, yet attacks them boldly & breathtakingly. Bill Wyman, moving with the times, wields one of those revolutionary slimline bass guitars you've seen on *TOTP*, but doesn't move much else, save for the occasional smug grin, or to light another in the incessant chain of ciggies. And then there's Jagger, crying out the pains & done-me-wrongs of two generations in his NY/UK hillbilly drawl.

His vital athleticism was unbounded & must be unparalleled. Tanned, with every ounce of excess fat stripped off, he pogo'd & beckoned, jerked about & sprang (not forgetting pouted) all over the shuddering shop right up until 'Honky Tonk Woman', 'Brown Sugar', 'Start Me Up' & yes 'Jumping Jack Flash' brought the show to a close. In fact, he looked somehow like a cartoon, in baggy blue knickerbockers & stripped off string vest. So did Woody, whose wild hair gradually saturated with sweat & deflated until it lay flat. And the guitarist's deep-set eyes added to the impression. I suppose them not being distant made their features seem exaggerated, as in comic strips. It would be nice if the Stones always played here. But then you could see why they're playing two nights at Wembley Stadium. Maybe the Pope should've tried going rock 'n' roll too.'

November 1982

Mick's relationship with Jerry Hall was going through a bad patch and the press picked up on it. This cartoon is from the *Daily Star*.

'It's not the end of the world, Mick, there's always Liz Taylor'

'It was Mick's 40th birthday – it answered what one journalist asked in 1969: "What can a Rolling Stone do at 40? It's the saddest thing in the world to contemplate a Rolling Stone in middle age."'

Douglas Hayward
Illustrated London News

'No trouble, Mr Jagger – PLENTY of people are sensitive about reaching F-O-R-T-Y'

'Entering his 40th year, Rolling Stone Mick Jagger celebrated with 50 friends into the early hours of yesterday at Langan's Brasserie off Piccadilly and revealed that scarlet-clad girlfriend Jerry Hall had given him an antique piece of furniture. Only one other Stone, Ronnie Wood, was at the bash and conspicuous by his absence was the group's financial adviser, royal friend Prince Rupert Loewenstein.'

Daily Mail

It was amazing after all those years that the papers were still obsessed with Mick's lips!

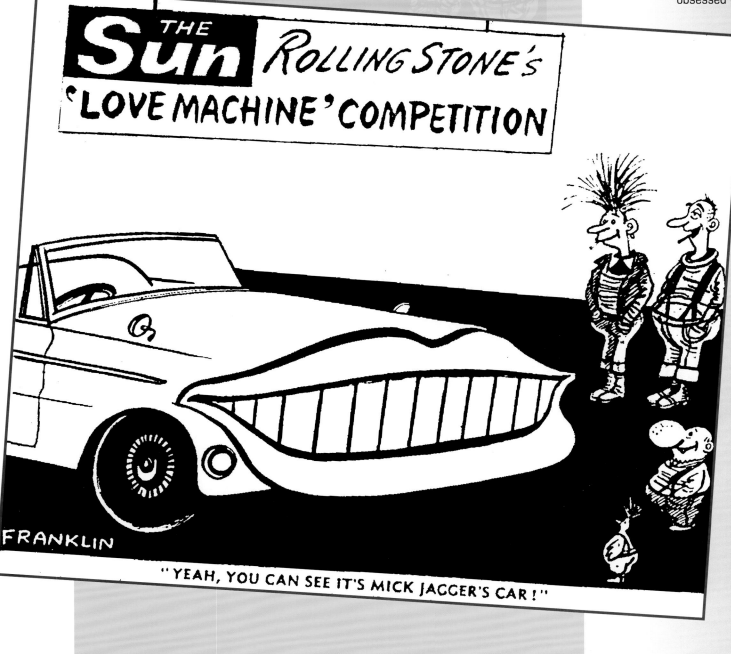

January 1984

Twenty years earlier we were touring the UK with The Ronettes, and only toured the US for the first time in June 1964. By the January of 1984 we had almost gone into hibernation as a band. We were all busy with our own projects and so it was nice to see we had not been forgotten.

"Do you realize the Rolling Stones have been together longer than we have?"

I wrote this for *The Children's Book* in aid of Save The Children's African Appeal.

RHYMIN' WYMAN

There once was a guy named Bill Wyman
  Who was not very hot with his rhymin'
He met a man named Brian Jones
  Who formed a band called the Stones
With a now-famous singer called Jagger

They played music all over the land
  And became the best rock 'n' roll band
Over sixty gold discs
  Topped the best-selling lists
For twenty-two years and still going

They were the first with long hair
  No stage clothes, at that time, was rare
But rebels they were then
  Five angry young men
And the press had the time of their lives

They came through it with a smile
  They've seen the world change to their style
Everyone knows them
  Wherever they go
And I can't rhyme this last line either!!

Bill Wyman

April 1985

I put out my own solo album in April 1985 – it harked back to one of my favourite bands, Creedence Clearwater Revival.

Steve Kingston, the artist who designed the cover for my solo album, also drew my Christmas card that year.

March 1988

We didn't see much of each other during 1987 and 1988, but I provided the *Sun* cartoonist with some inspiration. Somebody tried to talk me into starting a model agency business – which I did not pursue!

5th June 1988

According to the *Sunday Times*, 'Rock's hot legend rolls along into staid middle age.' It was all prompted by Mick's upcoming 45th birthday.

Sympathy for the capitalist: after 25 years, the Stones find satisfaction in business

9th March 1989

At 8.45 a.m. I drove to Gatwick Airport, and flew with British Airways to Barbados. I arrived at 6 p.m. (local time). At 7 p.m. I arrived at Ginger Bay Hotel and checked into Room 8. At 8.15 p.m. I went to Eddie Grant's studio, 'Blue Wave', and met up with everyone except Ronnie. We rehearsed from 10 p.m. to 12.30 a.m.

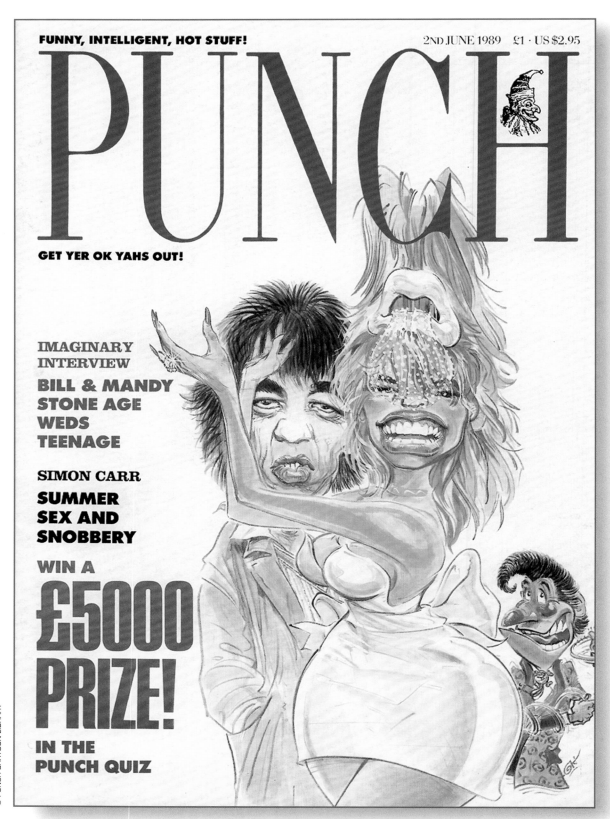

"How's married life? — Not so hot . . . Bill's got me ironing every night."

At 10.15 a.m. I and the rest of the Stones went on a private train to Grand Central station for a press conference at 12 noon to announce our US tour. It was to be our first US tour for eight years.

24th November 1989

By the time this caricature appeared we were three-quarters of the way through the US leg of our Steel Wheels tour. In all we played to over 3 million people in America and grossed $98 million, which was a lot of money. But then again everything about the tour was large, from the size of our touring party – the size of a small army – to the length of the set list. These two American caricatures show us in a very different light.

Nineties . . ■ ■ ■

When we finished the US tour we had six weeks off before we headed to Japan. This was our first tour of the country and it was not only one of the shortest tours we had ever undertaken, but also one of the most lucrative of our career. In actual fact it was not really a tour but ten shows in one place – Tokyo's Korakuen Dome. We were watched by half a million people on a tour sponsored by the oddly named, to western ears, Pocari Sweat – one of Japan's leading soft drinks.

After another couple of months off we toured Europe. Over 2 million fans saw us on the Urban Jungle tour, the change of name coming about because the stage set was smaller than the US Steel Wheels affair. We were criticised and accused of 'short changing' our European fans, but the fact was that the stadiums in Europe were generally much smaller than US venues. For the Wembley shows at the end of the tour we used the Steel Wheels set. These two tours were not my favourite time with the Stones. My Dad died while I was in Japan and my marriage was falling apart. Having said that, everyone from the band to the road crew was great, and despite everything we had some good laughs. On one gig the road crew got me a strip-o-gram, the only problem was she did it in the middle of the show, but she was under the stage where only I could see her! They wanted to see if I moved around while I played in order to get a better view!

In January 1991 we were back in the recording studio and soon rumours began appearing in the press about my leaving the band; and they were right. I had been contemplating this for a while and in the spring I decided I was going to leave. Apart from family and the band, no one else knew, and in truth

and Beyond

I think Mick and Keith thought 'I would come to my senses' and stay. But I was determined to do the things with my life that I wanted to do, and to prove that there was more to life, for me anyway, than just playing bass for the greatest rock 'n' roll band in the world. When I finally announced my departure in January 1993 it was like a weight being lifted from my shoulders. Not that anything really changed for the band; it was business as normal and a new tour began in the summer of 1994. The Stones' album Voodoo Lounge got to No. 1 in the UK, becoming the first to do so since 1980. In July 1995 I took my new wife Suzanne and our daughter Katie to see the Stones at Wembley. It was the first time I had seen them live and I really quite enjoyed it.

The Rolly Stokers, as the late great Stanley Unwin called the band, have continued to provide more in the way of inspiration for cartoonists than anyone in the music business. There have been more tours, more albums and of course Mick being knighted was, for the media as a whole, just like winning the lottery. As Keith told a magazine at the time, 'I don't want to step out onstage with someone wearing a coronet and sporting the old ermine. I told Mick it's a paltry honour. . . . It's not what the Stones is about, is it?' There's no doubt that none of us could ever have imagined what an amazing journey it was going to be.

In July 1962, a few months before I joined the band, Mick told *Jazz News*, 'I hope they don't think we're a Rock 'n' Roll outfit'. Well, Mick, Keith, Charlie, Woody, Brian, Mick T. and Stu, you were and you are – and I was proud to be a part of it.

1990

One of my favourite caricatures ever of the band didn't appear in print anywhere, as far as I know. I got it in unusual circumstances. It was purchased in a flea market in Seville, Spain, March 1993 by songwriter Pete Sinfield for 300 pesetas, and given to me with a note on the back saying 'Happy Birthday Sticky Fingers 2.7.97 – Why is Bill on a stick and why is Keith missing one eyebrow?' The artist appears to be A. Cadena.

'There has been wailing and gnashing of teeth by some rock critics as the Eighties have come under review. The main cause of the agony has been what might be called the Phil-Collinization of rock 'n' roll: the fact that the bulk of the biggest acts in the world are now middle-aged. It does not worry the general public much, but it worries writers who see it as an indication of falling standards and lost ideals. They think back to the days when singers had enough hair to consider a choice of styles, when fathers shouted 'turn that racket down', and local councils put bans on the music. Then they see Prince Charles shaking hands with nice guy Phil and they begin to weep. Why, oh why, they cry, are young people buying the music of a 50-year-old woman (Tina Turner) or a 40-year-old man (Bruce Springsteen)? Why did it have to be those 'wrinkle rockers', the Rolling Stones, who mounted the most lucrative tour of America last year? Why did Pete Townshend not expire painlessly before he got old? Oddly, the lament rarely extends to black male artists. There have been no calls for James Brown, now 56, to seek early retirement, and at 72 John Lee Hooker is counted a living legend. BB King had to wait until he was 64 to support U2 on tour.'

Steve Turner
The Times

Just after we had finished our huge US tour this piece appeared in the press. It's an fascinating comment on how times had changed, and an interesting contrast to the image on this US magazine cover of the Stones in the sixties.

26th May 1990

This caricature appeared in a Canadian magazine just as we were beginning the European leg of our tour, which had metamorphosed into the Urban Jungle tour.

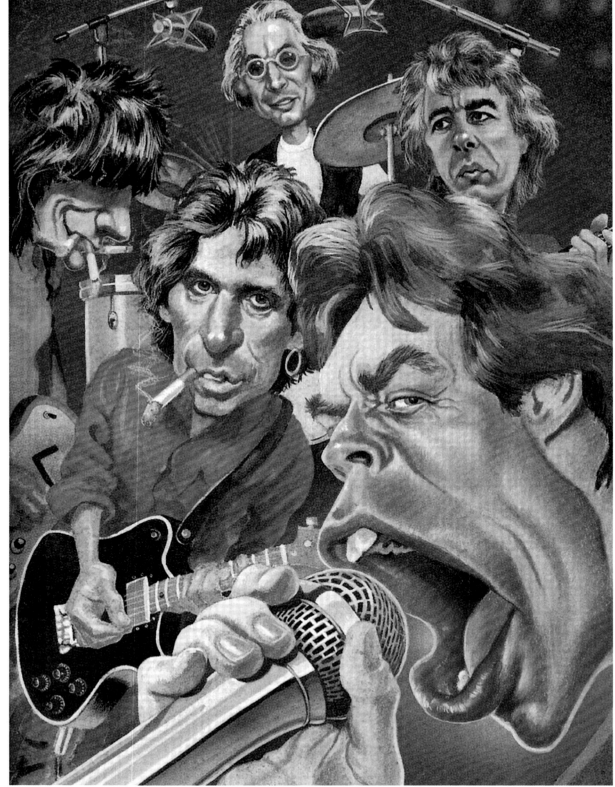

© STARWEEK, TORONTO

Our support band on the European tour was Gun, and one of its members drew these really good caricatures.

This cartoon of Mick appeared in *Punch* and apart from having Jerry Hall in the background it's interesting that it shows Mick in a tie – he'd come kind of full circle from the very early days of the band, when we still occasionally wore ties.

'You can picture Jagger picking at his smoked salmon and totting up the VAT while Keith sprawls across his bed and unstoppers the Rémy Martin. But this comically dissimilar pair give the Stones the sense of theatre which allows them to communicate in stadiums like this. In Sympathy For The Devil, Jagger suddenly appears like a gargoyle on the topmost level of the set while Richards slashes out chords several storeys below. The pair strut in front of the hideous inflatable woman-dolls of Honky Tonk Women, Jagger is swallowed by an inflatable Rottweiler in Street Fighting Man, and the duo out-prissy Julian Clary in a terrific Midnight Rambler. It was Keith who said, "I don't see why you can't have mature rock 'n' roll that can relate to young people as well as your own generation." Others try, but only these old blighters succeed.'

Adam Sweeting
The Guardian

When we played Wembley Stadium in July we were competing with the England football team, who were playing in the World Cup.

27th May 1991

In 1968 I wanted to buy a home in the country and through a good piece of fortune I went to look at Gedding Hall, near Bury St Edmunds in Suffolk. My girlfriend Astrid and I were shown around the grounds, by the gardener because the owner was away. A few days later we went back and met the owner, Geoff Allen, who showed us around the house, which was lovely. In the lounge I was shocked to see a signed photo of the Kray Brothers (Ronnie, Reggie and Charlie) on top of the TV. Geoff said they were great friends of his and often visited the Hall. I agreed to buy the Hall for £41,000, although Geoff told us that a member of the Queen's household was also interested, and he had offered more. Geoff said that he preferred to sell it to a self-made man, like himself.

© BURY TREE PRESS

138

"Excuse me, which one is mine?"

'Georgia May Ayeesha born to Mick and Jerry in London.'

August 1992

The papers were full of news of Mick and Jerry's marriage problems.

In July 1993 the press found yet another angle. Between these two views of Mick's marriage I left the Rolling Stones. I decided to make the announcement on the TV show *London Tonight*. The first mention here of Suzanne needs some explaining! I had met Californian Suzanne Accosta in Paris in the early eighties, when she was modelling. We had remained friends, and after my marriage to Mandy ended, Suzanne came over to London to visit me and found that we had something very special. I asked her to marry me and that's why you suddenly see marriage plans being referred to!

"Don't bother your father, Scarlett, he's not mature enough to build sandcastles!"

You're too late – he's doing his own kissagram

I woke up at 10.15 a.m., feeling tired. Suzanne went to the health club and I went back to sleep. I got up at 12.15 a.m. to an overcast day. At 1.15 p.m. I phoned Karen and discussed Press Release for Retirement from the Stones, dental check-ups and eye testing, fixing entrance TV monitor, checking our Sky TV receiver being repaired, and checked on our marriage plans for France. At 5 p.m. Suzanne and I left and went to ITV Studios, near Waterloo, where we met up with Matt Lorenzo.

I'm sure most people thought I would change my mind. But I was very happy with the choice I had made and I've never looked back, except with great affection for the great times that we had. Within two days of 'retirement' I was at my house in Suffolk working on an archaeological dig in the grounds — I was doing the things I wanted to do. Pretty soon though I started working on other projects and I've been busier since I left the Stones than I was when I was in the band!

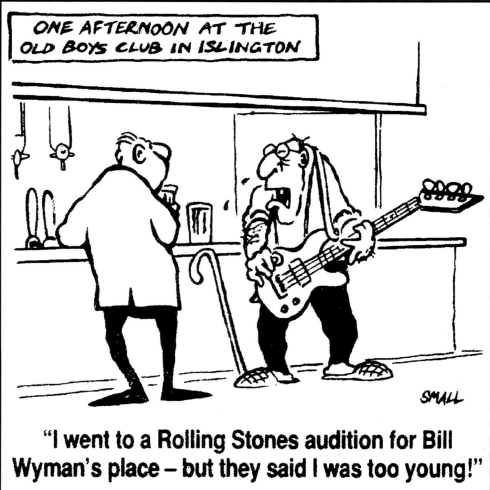

ONE AFTERNOON AT THE OLD BOYS CLUB IN ISLINGTON

SMALL

"I went to a Rolling Stones audition for Bill Wyman's place – but they said I was too young!"

July 1994

The Stones' new album, Voodoo Lounge, came out and as usual prompted some to see the funny side. The tour in support of the album got similar treatment.

Times had changed for the Stones, as you can see from this quote from a business magazine: 'The Rolling Stones – the former bad boys of rock 'n' roll – hardly fit the stereo-type of pinstriped marketing managers, but they're wearing the new role like their best pair of faded blue jeans. The Stones' plunge into direct marketing has incorporated a merchandise catalog, affinity credit cards, DRTV

MOTHER GOOSE & GRIMM

Mike Peters

AFTER AN ALL-NIGHT PARTY, MICK JAGGER'S MAID TRIES TO CLEAN UP ... LEAVING NO STONE UNTURNED.

and an address on the Internet. The group even has its own database. The 100,000-name fan file was compiled from concert attendees, merchandise buyers and fan-club members. Toronto-based Brockum Merchandising Co., exclusive merchandiser for the Stones and other groups, is using the database to promote upcoming Stones Voodoo Lounge tour.'

143

July 1995

By the time the Voodoo Lounge tour reached the UK the *Evening Standard* saw Mick and Keith in a very different light!

This wonderfully expressive caricature of Charlie reminds me of how it was to play alongside him all those years. I would look over and there would be Charlie laying down that rock solid beat, complemented by my bass. Even though I left the band Charlie and I have never stopped being great mates. He pops around to my house in Chelsea for a cup of tea, and never forgets to send my little girls T-shirts from the latest Stones tour.

One day I got a phone call from Charlie – the Stones were on tour. ''Ello Bill it's Charlie.' 'Where are you?' I asked. 'Hang on' (I heard Charlie going to the other side of the room and then coming back . . . he picks up the phone again), 'I'm in Buenos Aires. Anyway, Bill, tonight in the middle of the show I looked over to say something to you and you weren't there.'

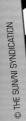

Mick was still getting into trouble with the press over his marital problems. I really like this one of Jerry with Mick on a lead – caught with his trousers down!

The next Stones' tour drove the cartoonists to even greater lengths in commenting about the age of the band.

'I think I'm going mad. Last week I saw Elvis and just now I could swear I saw the Rolling Stones'

1998

The Stones' massive earnings from touring brought about a repeat of the tax problems from the 1970s and with it a whole new look at the band.

© THE TIMES/NI SYNDICATION

SEX, DRUGS TAX AVOIDANCE AND ROCK N' ROLL

PUGH

© EXPRESS NEWSPAPERS

"Drug Squad? Cool! I thought you were the taxman."

I DON'T NEED NO SELF-ASSESSMENT

THEY'RE NOW INTO PROTEST SONGS

dave GASKILL

© THE SUN/NI SYNDICATION

'And on keyboard, tax consultant Kevin Botley.'

While the Stones were busy
touring the world, I was busy in
another, very different, field.

Meanwhile, Mick was facing up to the trials and tribulations of fatherhood.

1999

Mick's domestic life prompted yet another outpouring of the cartoonist's craft when he denied that he and Jerry were officially married.

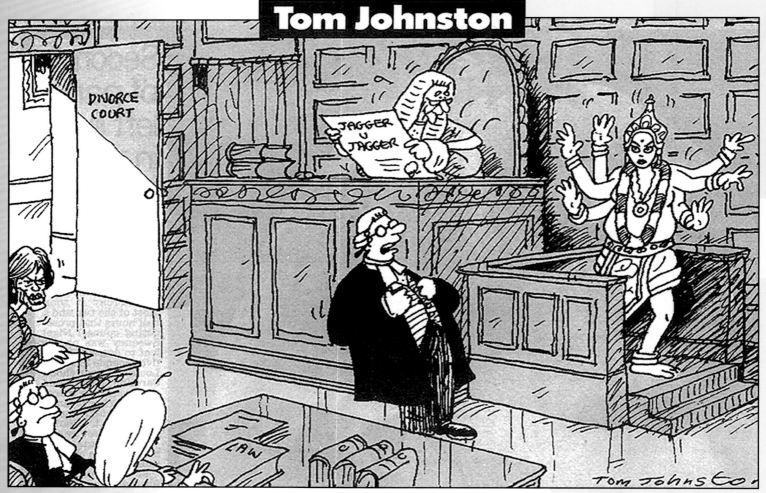

'Raise your right hands and tell us if Mick and Jerry had a proper Hindu wedding!'

2002

The Stones, well Mick to be precise, finally gained respectability when he became Sir Mick Jagger.

'After that performance, Mick, you rightly deserve a knighthood!'

'Mick's so pleased he's making a donation to the Labour Party – us!'

Mick and Keith remain the heart and soul of the Stones, even though Keith had gone on about Mick getting a knighthood – I don't know why Keith was so surprised. In 1974 Mick had told a journalist, 'A knighthood, I'd take, nothing less than a knighthood. But you gotta last a long time to get a knighthood.' Well, the Stones have lasted a long time, longer than any of us thought possible.

I hope they last forever.

During my 30 years in the Stones I was as often as not standing up the back with Charlie laying down that rock solid rhythm. This is how I remember Mick.

Acknowledgements

I would like to thank all the wonderful artists who have not only given permission for their cartoons and caricatures to be used in this book but also done such great work poking fun at us over the years. I should also perhaps thank the other Stones who provided inspiration – I'll include myself in that too!

A big thank you to Andrew for his brilliant foreword. His writing skills were in evidence on the back of the first Stones' album and the years have not dimmed his talents – they've honed them. Anyone with an interest in the Stones or the sixties should read Andrew's two books – *Stoned* and *2Stoned*; they are probably two of the best books on both subjects.

Andrew asked me to say thanks to 'al kooper for editing andrew, who has always needed editing'. He has a point.

Finally a big thank you to everyone involved with the project at Sutton Publishing. Jeremy Yates-Round had the vision to see how this project could work, and he's proved to be what can only be described as a model editor. Glad Stockdale has once again designed a great book for us – whatever Sutton pay her it's not enough. Nick Reynolds has brought order where there was order – order of a quite quiet kind. If you're reading this having bought the book then Jim Crawley has done his job well. If you haven't bought it yet, buy it and make Jim look good in the eyes of those who pay him. Juliet Davis, who cleared the permissions for the cartoons, faced a daunting task and we thank her for doing it so efficiently.

Suzanne and Christine have yet again suffered for our art . . . well something like that.

Bill Wyman, London
Richard Havers, the Scottish Borders
February 2006